USA

RED, WHITE, BLUE & GOLD
The U.S. Olympic Team at the
Games of the XXVII Olympiad

Editor/Publisher
Wallace Sears

Associate Editor
Kim Koenemann

Coordinators
Fran Henderson
Brad Sinclair

Special Editorial Assistance
Provided by U.S. Olympic Committee

Managing Director for Media & Public Affairs
Mike Moran

Director of Athlete Marketing
Barry King

Director of Media Services
Bob Condron

Book Designer
Terry Chandler

Photography
Allsport
London, New York, Los Angeles,
Sydney, Melbourne

Printing
American Printing Company, Inc.
Birmingham, Alabama

Pachyderm Press

Jamie Squire/Allsport

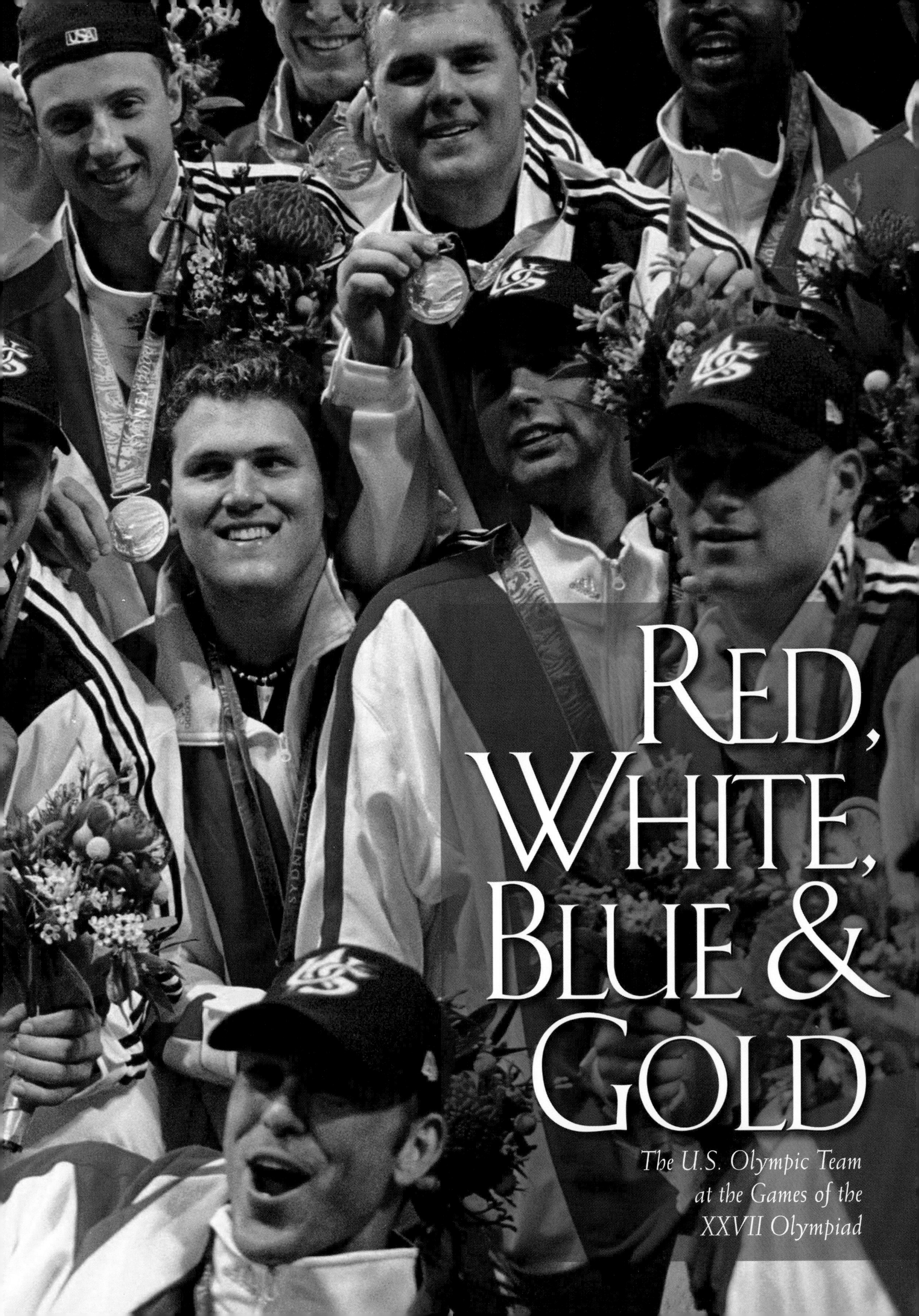

RED, WHITE, BLUE & GOLD

The U.S. Olympic Team
at the Games of the
XXVII Olympiad

SANDY BALDWIN
CHEF DE MISSION, U.S. OLYMPIC TEAM

Americans can be proud of the 2000 United States Olympic Team. These athletes were great representatives of our country and of their sports. This was a great group of ladies and gentlemen and we admire what they did in Sydney in what was called the best Olympic Games in history.

As chef de mission of the U.S. Olympic Team these athletes made my job easy. The 602 members of the U.S. Team led the medal count among all countries with 97 medals…40 of them gold. But, beyond medals, our athletes conducted themselves with class, just as they performed with class.

Again, we can be proud of what they did in Sydney and how they did it. We will be forever grateful for these memories in the final Games of the 20th Century.

BILL HYBL
PRESIDENT, U.S. OLYMPIC COMMITTEE

As we closed out one millennium and began another, we will never forget the Olympic Games of 2000 and the wonderful people of Australia. But, we also will never forget the performances of these 602 American men and women and how proud of them we were in these Games.

In years to come as we look back on these Games in this beautiful country we'll remember the moments of American greatness and the pride and exhilaration we took from these performances. We can be proud of these men and women. They were true ambassadors for our country.

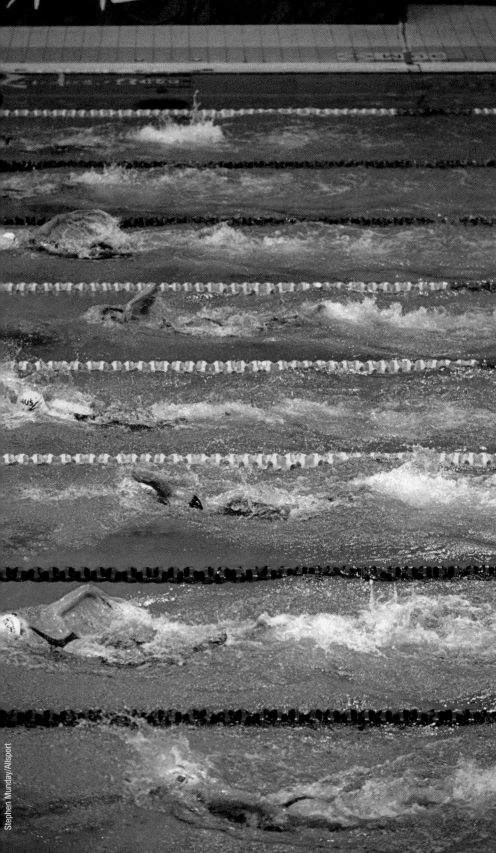

Stephen Munday/Allsport

Published under license from the U.S. Olympic Committee by:
Pachyderm Press, Inc., P. O. Box 661016, Birmingham, AL 35266-1016, 205/822-4139

The editorial materials contained in Red, White, Blue and Gold: The U.S. Olympic Team at the Games of the XXVII Olympiad are produced by Pachyderm Press, Inc. exclusively and are not the responsibility of the U.S. Olympic Committee.

U.S. Olympic Committee, One Olympic Plaza, Colorado Springs, CO 80909-5760, 719/632-5551

ISBN 0-9639505-6-8

TABLE OF CONTENTS

XXVII Olympiad 18
Competition. 34
  Archery 36
  Athletics 38
  Badminton. 52
  Baseball 54
  Basketball. 62
  Boxing 70
  Canoe/Kayak 74
  Cycling 78
  Diving 84
  Equestrian. 88
  Fencing 92
  Gymnastics. 94
  Judo. 102
  Modern Pentathlon 104
  Rowing 106
  Sailing 110
  Shooting 118
  Soccer. 122
  Softball. 128
  Swimming 134
  Synchronized Swimming . 150
  Table Tennis. 152
  Taekwondo. 154
  Tennis. 156
  Triathlon 160
  Volleyball 162
  Water Polo. 170
  Weightlifting. 174
  Wrestling. 178
Medals 186
Joy & Despair. 200
People. 210
Stars & Stripes 216
USOC Committee Members . 220
Results. 226
Roster 242
Staff 276

UNITED STATES OF AMERICA

XXVII
GAMES

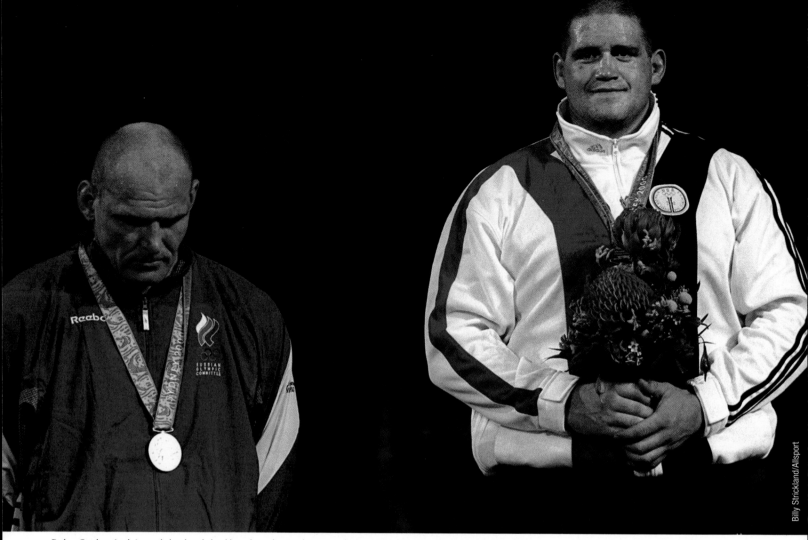

Rulon Gardner (right) stands head and shoulders above the man known as the greatest Greco-Roman Wrestler in the world, Alexander Karelin, after handing him the first defeat of his 13-year career.

XXVII OLYMPIAD

By Doug Looney

It was the perfect confluence of excellence between man and event.

Indeed, America's super heavyweight Greco-Roman wrestler Rulon Gardner and the 2000 Sydney Olympics go together like Rodgers and Hammerstein, dot and com, salt and pepper, buttons and bows, love and marriage, Abbott and Costello, ham and eggs, high and mighty, Bogey and Bacall, be and bop, kangaroos and hop...Help, can't stop.

It was a marriage made on the wrestling mat between Gardner, arguably the most unlikely gold medal winner for the U.S. in Olympic history, and Sydney, which put on such an exquisite Games that forevermore it will be intimidating to other cities and lands that follow as

hosts. Routinely, Sydney is voted the best city in the world by respected travel magazines. That's neither mistake nor fluke.

Gardner and Sydney define the other. Each gives better understanding of the other. Each glows because of the other.

Arm in arm, Gardner and Sydney set the bar way, way up there in the heavens.

At core, what Gardner and Sydney share is an indomitable spirit and can-do approach. "Believe in your mind," says Gardner, "and your body can do whatever it's asked to do." Indeed, they share that old-fashioned attitude that hard work with honest motives has a doggoned good chance of success—still.

Basically, what Gardner and Sydney are about is all that is good and great about the Olympics.

All Rulon Gardner did, of course, was defeat Russian Alexander Karelin. Karelin's resume was all wins—including 12 European championships, 9 world championships, 3 straight Olympic golds. He hadn't been beaten since 1987. U.S. coach Don Chandler says of Gardner, "He beat the greatest wrestler of all time."

And one of the greatest athletes of all time.

Conversely, Gardner's best ever finish in international competition was a fifth in the 1997 World Championships-getting beaten along the way 5-0, by Karelin. This is

An aerial view of Olympic Park in Homebush Bay showcases the centerpiece of Olympic venues.

heady stuff for a young man who grew up as one of nine children on a farm in Afton, Wyo. (pop: 1,394 exceptionally hearty souls) which everyone knows is just down the road from Grover and up the road from Smoot.

"I didn't actually think I could beat him," says Gardner, with that delightful brand of Wyoming candor and straightforwardness. "All I knew was that I'd go out with my head down and work forward....I always learned that when you work, you go forward. I've had practice in pushing cows and (Karelin's) like that, but he's a little quicker."

Afton Mayor Jerry Hansen told the Associated Press, "This is probably the greatest thing in the valley since the first settlers survived early winters."

If the U.S. could have picked a better representative-yea, a better symbol-for all that was marvelous about Sydney and the Olympics, it could have done no better than Gardner. "The pride has not left me from the moment I won the gold medal," he says. When Gardner was

picked to be the American flag bearer at the Closing Ceremony, he had the perfect response: "Wow." He went on to say "it makes me feel honored to be an American." This is all cherry pie and Norman Rockwell and red, white and whew.

And Wyoming cowboy.

It takes us back to the '50s-come on, how many Olympic heroes spent endless hours milking cows and baling hay?—when things were more simple.

But what made the Olympics dazzle goes far beyond the exquisite Gardner-Sydney tableau.

The U.S. athletes were-to understate-their typically wondrous selves. The team won 97 medals to once again lead all nations. Forty of the medals were everyone's favorite color. Russia was second with 88 medals, China third with 59.

In one of this country's signature sports, the American swimmers approached water's edge with a certain confidence-as well they should. It is never, ever bragging when you can back it up. When all the splashing stopped at the Aquatic

Center, Australian swim coach Don Talbot conceded, "The rest of the world is still trying to catch the U.S."

The proof is always in the numbers: The U.S. swimmers won 33 medals. Australia was second with 18.

Lenny Krayzelburg won two individual gold medals, in the 100- and 200-meter backstroke, with Olympic records in both. Tom Dolan set a world record in the 400-meter individual medley and definitely got it right when he said afterwards that as an American, "You walk in the room and other swimmers fear you." Jenny Thompson won three more golds in relays, giving her a career total of eight-and making her the most gold bedecked female U.S. Olympic athlete ever. Gary Hall and Anthony Ervin tied for gold in the 50-meter freestyle, an Olympic rarity. Hall, the favorite, was gracious: "I don't mind sharing the gold medal platform at all."

Brooke Bennett won the 800- meter freestyle, wiping out the Olympic record set by the legendary Janet Evans in 1988, and the 400- meter freestyle. Bennett, like Rulon

Gardner, had the right-on response: "I'm so proud of myself."

Who, pray tell, wouldn't be?

Who, pray tell, wouldn't deserve to be?

And it wasn't just U.S. swimmers covering themselves in glory. No more jokes, please, about Holland being only a land of tulips and windmills. Dutch swimmer Inge de Bruijn won three golds, all in world record times. Pieter van den Hoogenband won two golds in world times and added a bronze. All of this added new meaning to Dutch masters.

This brings us to Marion Jones, who added new meaning to setting high goals. Nothing could be more in line with Olympic thought. Jones surveyed the scene months ahead of time and promptly announced her plan was to win five gold medals.

Did she really think she could pull off such an audacious idea? "I don't handle failure very well," she answered.

As it turned out, Jones failed – by her measure. All she did was demolish the field in winning both the 100- and 200-meters and add another win with her blazing leg on a relay team. But she couldn't get off a distant enough and legal enough long jump, ending third, and through no fault of hers, ran on another relay team that finished third.

Scott Barbour/Allsport

Jed Jacobsohn/Allsport

Top: Cengiz Koc of Germany is knocked out in the first round by Alexis Rubalcaba Polleda of Cuba.

Middle: Fireworks punctuate the opening of the 2000 Sydney Olympics as the Olympic Flame is raised to the top of Olympic Stadium

Right: Haile Gebrselassie of Ethiopia, unbeaten in seven years in the event, beats longtime rival Paul Tergat of Kenya to the tape by only nine hundredths of a second and wins the 10,000 meter gold medal.

Next page: Skipper Paul Foerster, 1992 Flying Dutchman silver medalist, and Robert Merrick paired to bring the U.S. a silver medal in 470-class sailing.

Mike Hewitt/Allsport

Darren England/Allsport

Adam Pretty/Allsport

IOC President Juan Antonio Samaranch echoes the excitement of the Games as he joins "the wave" during the beach volleyball gold medal match between Brazil and the U.S.

Romanian Gabriela Szabo makes her move on Gete Wami in the 5000-meter race.

Left: Karin Ertl of Germany shows graceful form in the javelin discipline of the heptathlon competition.

Total: Three golds and two bronzes. That this was somehow disappointing speaks volumes about Jones' talent. She is, after all, still the first woman to ever win five medals in track and field in a single Olympics.

But that Jones had the courage to think beyond simply winning to flaming excellence riveted the world's attention. No mountain is too high for a climber, and for anyone else to have suggested five golds would have been nonsense.

Ultimately, all it meant for Jones was that her reach exceeded her grasp. So?

She left Sydney the same heroine that she arrived as. Typically, there were no excuses. At Games' end, she was classy, dignified, and unbowed, telling NBCOlympics.com, "I wanted to come here and win everything."

That's what we wanted, too. But she was a long, long way from being viewed as chopped liver when all the cheering stopped.

Yet, to suggest that track and field was all about Jones would do a disservice to amazing performances by a flock of others.

It's probably true-albeit arguable-that the No. 1 event in any Olympics is the men's 100-meter. The winner instantly becomes known as The World's Fastest Human. Prior to running in Sydney, Maurice Greene insisted, "I am not afraid of anyone." With that, he promptly put all his competitors in the shade with yet another blurry fast performance.

The third major story in track and field was Michael Johnson, who says he thinks of himself as "hard, cold steel." In no way did he bend, winning the 400-meters with ease in what he says is his last major

individual competition.

There was hope that Johnson might be able to better his own world record, but cool, breezy, damp conditions precluded it. Johnson, however, never loses focus on the big picture: "It's about winning, not times." He is the first to repeat as Olympic 400 champ.

Going into the Olympics, there were many questions across the American landscape. To wit:

• Would a U.S. baseball team composed of minor leaguers be able to even medal in the Games, much less win gold against highly regarded Cuba? You betcha.

It was as if manager Tommy Lasorda, former Dodger manager, willed it so. Never mind the Cubans had won every Olympic and World title since 1969. Early on, it seemed as if Lasorda was whistling past the cemetery when he said of his team,

23

Jed Jacobsohn/Allsport

Darren England/Allsport

Above: Lucien James "Luc" Longley, the first Australian to play in the NBA and winner of three NBA titles with the Chicago Bulls, took time off from his new team, the New York Knicks, to play for his home team in the Sydney Games.

Above right: Australian heroine Cathy Freeman easily wins gold in the 400-meter race to the screams of nearly 110,000 fans in Olympic Stadium.

Right: The cauldron containing the Olympic Flame rises out of the water and above torchbearer Cathy Freeman on its way to its home atop Olympic Stadium where it remains for the next 15 days.

Below left: Australian Ian Thorpe, the "Thorpedo," backs up his claim to fame winning the 400-meter freestyle race and smashing the world record in the process.

Below right: Australian Tatiana Grigorieva knows the only way to beat Stacy Dragila of the United States for the gold is to go for the world record. She missed her attempt and finished with the silver medal.

Billy Strickland/Allsport

Nick Wilson/Allsport

Mike Powell/Allsport

"They're going to want it more than the other team and that's the way we're going to win."

The Americans throttled Cuba 4-0 in the gold medal game. How? They wanted it more.

Lasorda added enormously to the Games with his optimism, his exuberance, and his devotion: "This is bigger than the World Series. This is bigger than the Dodgers. It's bigger than major league baseball." Ah, Tommy, this is why we love you.

• Would the U.S. women's basketball team have enough of everything to keep it together against the talented Australians, supported by fans that give screaming meaning to fanatical? You betcha.

The U.S. handled the Aussies easily in the final, 76-54. Said coach Nell Fortner, "You don't know what you have learned until you are in the position to use it." Once again, clearly, when students are ready to learn, a teacher appears.

• Coming into an Olympic contest against Japan, the U.S. women softballers had won 112 straight. They lost. They lost again. They lost a third time. It clearly looked to be an inexplicable debacle a-borning. Was there even a long shot hope they could right this floundering ship? You betcha.

Somehow and some way, the team was able to dig deep within itself and, on a rainy night in Sydney, beat Japan 2-1 for the gold on a fly ball error by the losers. The triumph was more about character and perseverance than about pure sport.

Competitors in the women's marathon cross the world's largest steel arch bridge, Sydney Harbor Bridge.

"We've won, we've won," hollered catcher Stacey Nuveman. She sounded in shock.

• Could Stacy Dragila withstand the pressure of being an over-the-top favorite to win the women's pole vault in the sport's Olympic debut? You betcha.

Dragila, who formerly excelled in rodeo goat-tying, said of the public enthusiasm for the event, "We're dang exciting."

• Could the men's basketball Dream Team, such a huge favorite that conventional wisdom was it could win blindfolded, ever be motivated enough to win gold? You betcha.

There was a narrow win over Lithuania and a less than dominating win in the final over France. Still, there was an underlying feeling that the NBA stars could always ratchet things up just enough to get by. Vin Baker called the win "the best moment I've ever had as a basketball player."

But there's no question the rest of the world is improving at hoops. So in the future, a dozy effort by the U.S. could spell trouble. But in Sydney, no worries, as the life-loving Aussies say.

And it's worth noting the average margin of victory for the U.S. was still above 20 points.

• Could U.S. diver Laura Wilkinson, who broke her foot in three places earlier this year in training, conquer any residual fears? You betcha.

All she did was approach the task with enormous aplomb and become the first U.S. woman diver to win off the 10-meter platform in 36 years.

• Could the men's soccer team possibly have any success? You betcha.

In a performance that far exceeded expectations, the Americans advanced to the semifinals for the first time in their Olympic history. Ultimately, they narrowly missed a medal, losing in the bronze game to Chile.

This is a huge kick forward.

HRH Princess Ann presents Great Britain's cyclists Rob Hayes (left) and Jonathan Clay with their bronze medals.

A U.S. outfielder stands in the light of the setting sun during a preliminary round game.

A competitor is caught mid-air in the first Olympic trampoline competition.

The jumbo screen catches the concentration of Svetlana Kazanina of Kazakhstan for all 110,00 fans in Olympic Stadium to see as she prepares for the javelin throw.

Soccer player Lauren Mayer Etame (#12) of Cameroon and his teammates are overjoyed at winning the first gold medal in history for their country.

*Photographers swarm around Marion Jones as she displays
the flags of her country, the U.S., and her mother's, Belize,
after she won her first gold medal in the 100-meter race.*

Billy Strickland/Allsport

In the past, people could hardly talk about the soccer team for giggling at its ineptitude. No more.

Coach Clive Charles calls the achievement "unbelievable." He understates.

And, as is so often the case, there was plenty of success in the failures. It truly is not the medal but the mettle.

For example, the storied U.S. women's soccer team got beat in overtime by Norway, 3-2, for the gold medal. Certainly the players had hoped for better. Said Brandi Chastain: "I think the expectation everyone puts on us can't possibly be as high as those we put on ourselves."

But along the way, coach April Heinrichs noted that her team never quits and "we find a way to win." One out of two isn't terrible.

Badminton player Kevin Han immigrated to this country from

Eric "The Eel" Moussambani of Equatorial Guinea became an instant celebrity when he refused to give up in one of the slowest races in Olympic history. Moussambani, who only learned to swim a few months before the Games, thought at one point that he might drown, but was spurred on to the finish by the overwhelming crowd support.

Nick Wilson/Allsport

Great Britain is greeted by a fan after winning gold in the Men's Coxless Four Rowing Final.

Top left: A competitor flies through his routine in the men's gymnastics floor exercise.

Top right: Australian comedic sports commentators Roy Slaven and H.G. Nelson emcee the beginning of the Closing Ceremony.

Center: Hungarian Balazs Kovacs stares down the track as he prepares to start the 110-meter hurdles.

Left: Chie Sieke of Japan signals her partner during women's beach volleyball.

31

Shanghai as a teenager. He found work as a busboy/delivery boy at a New York Chinese restaurant, learning quickly how to cope with mean streets. He lost in the round-of-16 in Sydney but the smile of gratitude remains. Han calls his 11 years in the U.S. where he has gone from busboy to national champ "an amazing ride."

Celebrity cyclist Lance Armstrong couldn't crank it up enough to win a gold medal. But he was sport enough to come to the South Pacific, give it a good go, and at least wind up with a bronze. More importantly, his oft-told, feel-wonderful story of fighting back against cancer added gloriously to the Olympic concoction.

It is easy to make snide fun of the Olympic theory that the important thing is the taking part, not the winning. Yeah, sure, show us a loser and we'll show you a loser.

Yet, it really is the taking part.

In a perverse way, Rulon Gardner was joined in defining these Olympics by Equatorial Guinea swimmer Eric Moussambani. He ended up swimming a qualifying heat by himself, the other competitors being disqualified. Moussambani had never swum the 100-meter freestyle, but was allowed to compete under a special Olympic provision to encourage participation by as many nations as possible.

He floundered, gasped, flailed, and barely made it with a time more than 50 seconds slower than the next slowest.

The crowd, of course, loved him. It was reminiscent of legendary Eddie "The Eagle" Edwards, the perfectly awful ski jumper in the 1988 Winter Olympics who won hearts because he tried.

Moussambani was ecstatic to have taken part. "I'm going to call my mother," he said afterwards, "then dance and jump."

The incredible Australian aboriginal runner, Cathy Freeman, defined her nation. She lit the

Australian golfer Greg "The Shark" Norman atop a giant shark joins other Australian icons in the Closing Ceremony.

Autralian supermodel Elle MacPherson parades around the track at the Closing Ceremony on top of a giant camera.

Olympic torch, she won the 400-meters, she moved the world. "I live for the moment," she says. What incredible moments. Without Freeman taking part-ignore the winning-the Olympics would have been far less.

No athlete who marched into Olympic Stadium with all the other athletes could have missed the elation

of taking part. There was drama and there was action and there was Olivia Newton John rocking that house in song.

While there often were tears on the medal stand-including American tennis star Venus Williams who won two golds-there also were tears from those competitors who didn't win but who realized taking part was a

An F-111 with after-burners blazing streaks across the night sky over Sydney Harbor symbolically carrying away the Olympic Flame to close the Games.

"Crocodile Dundee" star Paul Hogan waves to the athletes while riding a float shaped like his famous hat in the Closing Ceremony.

shining moment on the hill for them. Tears don't have to be bitter. They can be in gratitude. And they were.

Tears can be in joy, too. And they were. Anyone who sat at the Closing Ceremony and witnessed the F-111 jet scream over Olympic Stadium at 500 feet, symbolically carrying the Olympic flame off into the night sky with the afterburners roaring had to be moved to tears. It was required.

Rulon Gardner-"Dreams do come true," he sighs—had never seen anything like this in Wyoming while he was milking cows. But, in fairness, nobody else had ever seen anything like this either.

And down around Sydney Harbor-glorious Sydney Harbor-with the lights changing colors inside the Opera House and glitter everywhere across the water and the Olympic rings up on the harbor bridge, it is implausibly idyllic.

Ahhh, life is good.

It was a celebration for the ages.

USA

Author Douglas S. Looney is a former senior writer at Sports Illustrated, where he worked for more than 21 years. He lives in Colorado and was in Sydney for the Olympic Games.

COMPETITION

Rodney White takes aim to help clinch the bronze medal in men's Team competition.

ARCHERY

By Bill Kellick

The U.S. men's archery team brought home silver and bronze medals while the women's archery team was thwarted by the luck of the draw.

MEN
Competing in his first Olympic Games, Vic Wunderle of Mason City, IL, captured the silver medal in the men's individual competition. Wunderle also helped the U.S. men take the bronze medal in the team event.

The competition began with the ranking round after which Rod White of Mt. Pleasant, IA, was seeded fourth. Wunderle ranked seventh while the

third member of the U.S. team, Richard "Butch" Johnson of Woodstock, CT, struggled with the windy conditions and placed 31st heading into the elimination round. The U.S. men's team was seeded second for the team round behind top-ranked Korea.

The men's individual event got underway with all three American archers advancing past the first round. White and Johnson then ran into trouble as the winds increased and they were forced to make adjustments to both their form and timing. The lone U.S. archer to advance to the round-of-16 was Wunderle.

The scene was set for Wunderle to medal in his first Olympic Games. Two straight wins would put him in the medal round. Three wins would earn a berth in the gold medal match and four would give him the gold.

Wunderle defeated Vadim Shikarev of Kazakhstan and second-seeded Kyo-Moon Oh of Korea in the quarterfinals. Besting Sweden's Magnus Petersson, Wunderle moved on to the gold-medal final against Australia's Simon Fairweather.

Fairweather did not disappoint his home crowd, clinching the gold medal. Wunderle took the silver medal and Weitse van Alten of Holland earned

A steady hand, a strong arm and an eagle eye will guide Karen Scavotto's arrow to the target.
Below: At a distance of nearly 300 feet, the target appears to this archer to be about the size of a pencil eraser held at arm's length.

bronze. In team competition, the U.S. set an Olympic record of 255 points in its opening match against Sweden. After losing to Italy in the semifinals, the U.S. team captured the bronze medal in a heart-stopping shoot-out against Russia.

WOMEN

The women's competition began with Janet Dykman of El Monte, CA, placing 16th in the ranking round. Teammates Karen Scavotto of Enfield, CT, and Denise Parker of Salt Lake City, UT, placed 22nd and 43rd, respectively. Those seedings meant Scavotto and Parker would face each other in the first round, with only the winner advancing.

Scavotto began the individual elimination round with a win over teammate Parker. Dykman lost her first-round match to Australian Michelle Tremelling. It was left to 18-year-old Scavotto to carry the hopes of

the American women in the individual competition. Scavotto pulled out a tight victory over Yaremis Perez Ruiz of Cuba in the second round, but fell to Japan's Sayoko Kawauchi. The Korean women swept the individual competition taking gold, silver and bronze.

Luck of the draw was not with the U.S. women's team at these Games, facing eventual gold medalist Korea early in the competition. The U.S. won its first-round match over Sweden, but fell to Korea, which scored an Olympic record of 252 points.

The U.S. women's team finished the Games in fifth place having the highest score among the four losing teams in the quarterfinals. In fact, the U.S. score was higher than two of the four winning teams in the quarterfinals and could have battled for bronze were it not for drawing an early match with Korea.

Marion Jones wins gold in the women's 100-meter final and is on her way to becoming the most decorated woman in history of track and field at one Olympic Games.

ATHLETICS

USA

By Jill M. Geer

Established stars and fresh young talent combined efforts within the Mondo-surfaced confines of Olympic Stadium to yet again make Team USA the World's No.1 Track and Field team at the 2000 Sydney Olympic Games.

Winning more gold medals than the second- and third-best countries combined, Team USA easily topped the competition with 20 medals, 10 gold, four silver and six bronze, for its best showing at an international competition in the last four years.

Marion Jones became the most decorated woman in history at a single Olympics, winning five medals. She started the Games off

with huge wins in the 100- and 200-meters, then added bronze in the long jump and 4x100-meter relay before turning in the most dominant leg of the competition in the 4x400-meter relay to lead the U.S. to gold in that event.

Michael Johnson, who plans to retire from the sport in 2001, finished his Olympic career with two more gold medals, winning the 400-meters and running anchor on the 4x400-meter relay. Maurice Greene won double gold in his first Olympic Games, winning the 100-meters and running anchor on the 4x100-meter relay.

Twenty-one-year-old Angelo Taylor also won two golds for Team

USA, winning the 400-meter hurdles and running the first two rounds of the 4x400-meter relay.

Stacy Dragila made history by winning gold in the first Olympic women's pole vault, while compatriot Nick Hysong brought the U.S. its first gold in the men's pole vault since 1968.

The United States won three gold and one bronze medal to nearly sweep the relay competition.

FRIDAY, SEPTEMBER 22
Team USA's shot put throwers got the medal haul under way on the first day of track and field competition. Adam Nelson threw 21.21 meters (69 feet,

Michael Johnson becomes the first man in history to defend Olympic gold in the 400-meters.

Stacy Dragila clears the bar to become the first Olympic women's pole vault gold medalist.

7 inches) and John Godina, the 1996 silver medalist, was a centimeter behind at 21.20 meters (69' 6.25") to win silver and bronze, behind upset winner Arsi Harju of Finland (21.29 m/ 69' 10.25"). American Andy Bloom threw a strong 20.87 meters (68' 5.75") for fourth.

In a year that has seen him improve his personal best by nearly five feet, Nelson won his first-ever medal in a major championship. "This is my first major championship, and this is the biggest meet in the world," Nelson said. "I'm happy tonight."

SATURDAY, SEPTEMBER 23
Jones and Greene wasted no time in winning the first track and field golds of the Games for the United States. In the second day of competition, both sprinters, Jones, a two-time world champion and Greene, a two-time world champ and the world record holder, dominated the women's and men's 100-meters, respectively.

Jones beat the field by an astonishing .37 seconds, running 10.75 seconds to 11.12 for second-place finisher Ekaterini Thanou of

Greece. Greene got off to a modest start, then blasted the field with a 9.87 clocking. Ato Boldon of Trinidad & Tobago was second in 9.99. American Jon Drummond was a close fourth in 10.08.

Jones' time was the second fastest in Olympic history behind Florence Griffith Joyner's 1988 time of 10.62 seconds, and was the fastest time in the world this year. Jones and Greene both wept tears of joy after their performances.

"I've dreamed about this for 19 years," Jones said. "It was an

incredible
everything
and more."

SUNDAY,
Both of th
United Sta
significanc
night that
medals. M
first man e
an Olymp
meters, an
came in th
women's p

Johnso
final 150 m
seconds. A
Harrison w
seconds, in
place finis

"I felt w
performan
whose five
gold. "My
to make hi

Dragila
world reco
Australian
Vala Flosa
pole vault
winning h
feet, 1 inch
Grigorieva
Flosadottir

"This i
me," Dragi
medal take
anything I
to chose b
and setting

Jearl Miles-Clark passes the baton to Monique Hennagan on their way to the gold in women's 4x100-meter relay.

Mike Powell/Allsport

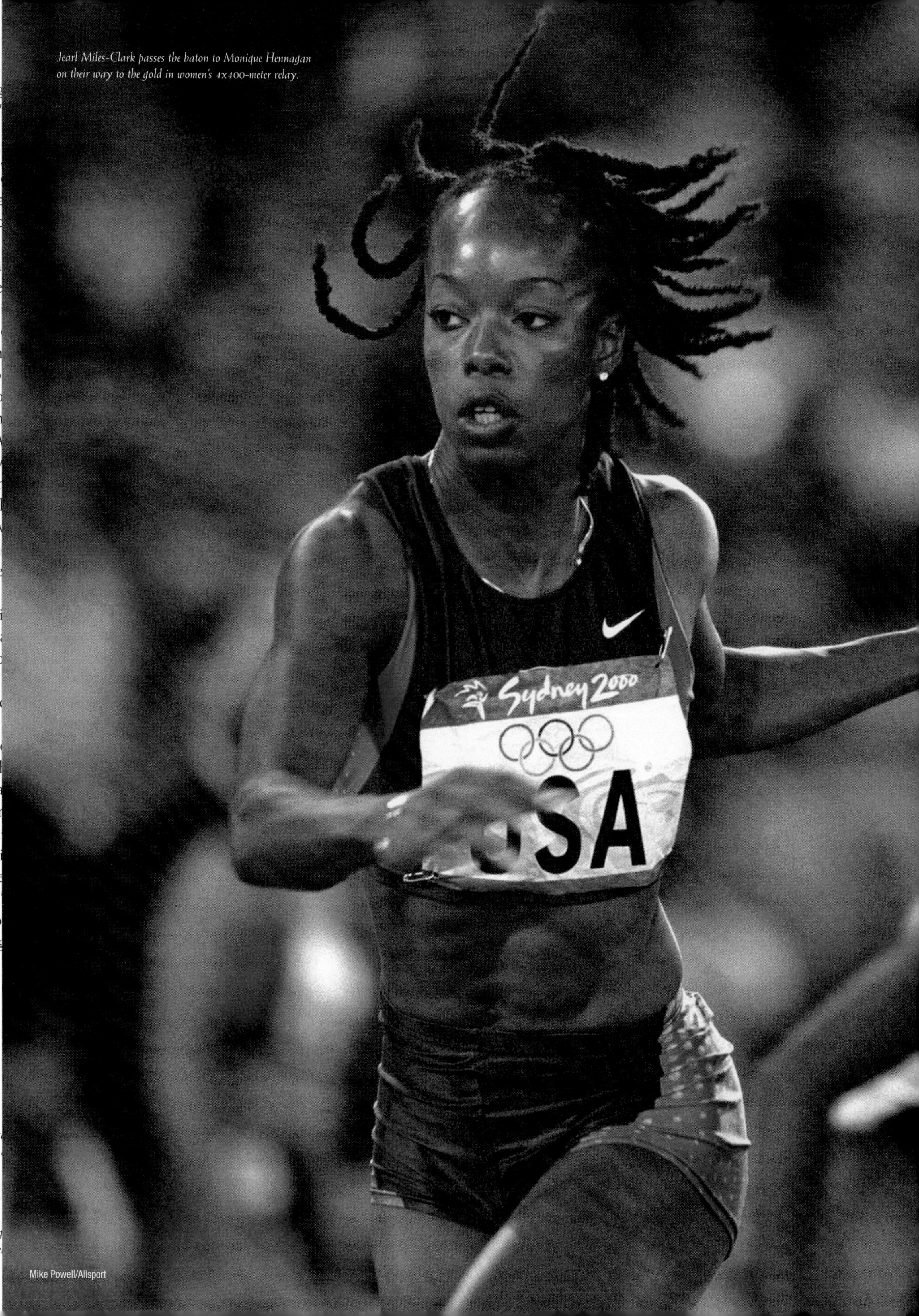

Chris Huffins st
Decathlon with

Adam Nelson is
of the men's shot

Angelo Taylor g
hurdles as Pawe

LaTasha Colander-Richardson crosses the line for gold in the final leg of the 4x400-meter relay.

Eric Thomas clears a hurdle on his way to the semifinal round of men's 400-meter hurdles.

Coming off the last hurdle, I just gave it all I had."

After a strong start, Morrison held on for third in the 100-meter hurdles in 12.76. Olga Shishigina of Kazakhstan won the race in 12.65, with Glory Alonzie of Nigeria second in 12.68.

THURSDAY, SEPTEMBER 28

Marion Jones won her second gold medal of the Olympic Games in much the same way as she won her first, by dominating the competition. Jones won the 200-meters in 21.84 seconds, her best time of the season, to finish ahead of Pauline Davis-Thompson of the Bahamas (22.27).

Chris Huffins added bronze for the United States in the decathlon. Finishing the two-day, 10-event competition in his least-beloved event, the 1500-meters, Huffins ran 4:38.71 to hold on for the bronze medal with 8595 points and set a personal best in the race by 13 seconds.

"For me to win an Olympic medal based on my 1500 means more to me than you'll ever be able to write about," Huffins told the media. "That's the event that has been my Waterloo so many times in my career. And for it all to come down to that and for me to dig deep inside my soul and come up with that kind of performance — that is my Olympic moment, now and forever."

FRIDAY, SEPTEMBER 29

Nick Hysong won Team USA's first gold in the pole vault since 1968 and Lawrence Johnson captured silver in the event. Marion Jones won her third medal of the Games with a bronze in the women's long jump in another successful night for USA track and field performers.

Hysong, who has never placed higher than second at the U.S.

Championships, won with a personal-best clearance of 5.90 meters (19' 4.25") to match Bob Seagren's golden achievement of 22 years ago. Hysong suffered only one miss in the course of the competition, at the second height of 5.70 meters (18' 8.5"). Johnson, the Olympic Trials champion and 1997 World Championships silver medalist, also cleared 5.90 meters with one miss at 5.90 meters, but Hysong earned the victory by virtue of clearing 5.90 meters on his first attempt. World Champion Maksim Tarasov of Russia was third at 5.90 meters with three misses.

"I feel awesome. It's just incredible," Hysong said. "My dream has always been to come to the Olympics and jump as I have. I can say that I accomplished that dream."

Jones posted just two legal jumps in the women's long jump competition, finishing third with a

Jamie Squire/Allsport

Ross Kinnaird/Allsport

Marion Jones is congratulated by Australian Olympic icon Cathy Freeman for her golden performance in the 200-meters.

Gabriel Jennings in the semifinal round of the 1500-meters.

mark of 6.92 meters. Heike Drechsler of Germany won with 6.99 meters (22' 11.25") and Fiona May of Italy was second at 6.92 meters, beating out Jones by having a second-best mark of 6.82 meters (22' 4.5") to Jones' 6.68 meters (21' 11").

"I thought I would come out here and win the gold," Jones said. "But you have to applaud Heike Drechsler. She was the better jumper today. I can tell my grandkids in 30 years that I competed against one of the best long jumpers ever."

Saturday, September 30

Team USA emerged from Olympic Stadium with three more gold medals and one bronze in relay events to put the final touches on the United States' 20-medal Olympic total, and Marion Jones emerged as the most decorated woman in a single Olympics in history.

The men's and women's 4x400-meter relays and the men's 4x100-meter relay won gold and the women's 4x100-meter relay took the bronze. Jones ran anchor leg on the 4x100 and ran a blistering third leg on the 4x400 to earn her fourth and fifth medals of the 2000 Olympic Games.

Jones' five medals surpass the performance in a single Olympics by Americans Florence Griffith Joyner (1988) and Fanny Blankers-Koen of the Netherlands (1948), both of whom won four.

The USA men's 4x100-meter relay of Jon Drummond, Bernard Williams, Brian Lewis and Maurice Greene won the first gold of the night on Saturday. With solid handoffs and a third leg by Lewis that put the team firmly in control of the race, Team USA won going away in 37.61. Brazil was second in 37.90 and Cuba was third in 38.04.

Suzy Favor Hamilton takes the lead in the women's 1500-meters and qualifies second for the final.

"The most important thing is to bring home the gold," Greene said. "I've always said I want to bring the United States back on top (in sprinting), and now that the relay gold is back in the United States, I believe it's here."

In the women's 4x100-meter relay, the USA combination of Chryste Gaines, Torri Edwards, Nanceen Perry and Marion Jones finished third in 42.20 seconds, with the Bahamas first in 41.95 and Jamaica second in 42.13. An ill-timed handoff from Edwards which caused Perry to slow and eventually turn around to get the baton proved too big a margin to make up even for Jones, who took the baton in fifth place and was closing hard on Jamaica at the finish for the bronze.

Jones returned to the track less than two hours later to join Jearl Miles-Clark, Monique Hennagan and LaTasha Colander-Richardson on the 4x400-meter relay. Miles-Clark (51.1 split) had a slight lead after the first leg, and USA and Jamaica were roughly even when Hennagan (51.4) handed off to Jones for the third leg. After a controlled first 150 meters, Jones built a huge lead in the last 200 meters and ran 49.4 seconds for her leg. Colander-Richardson (50.7) extended that lead in the first 300 of the anchor leg, and then held on to win in 3:22.62. Jamaica was second (3:23.25) and the Russian Federation was third (3:23.46).

Michael Johnson leaves the competition behind to take gold in the men's 400-meters.

Coby Miller advances from the heats to an eventual seventh place finish in the final of the 200-meters.

Previous page: Michael Johnson wins the last 400-meter Olympic gold medal of his career.

Maurice Greene is a blur as he passes through the heats on his way to the 100-meter final.

Shaun Botterill/Allsport

Michael Steele/Allsport

Pascal Dobert gives an Olympic effort in the 3000-meter steeplechase.

Adam Pretty/Allsport

Maurice Greene takes a stroll down the track before his first Olympic competition.

Anthony Washington in action in the Discus qualifying round.

"This is the Olympic Games; you've got to put it on the line," said Miles-Clark, who anchored the United States to gold at the 1996 Atlanta Olympics. "I told (Jones) that was one of the smoothest legs in the 400 I've ever seen. I was just happy she was on my team."

With a win in the men's 4x400-meter relay, Michael Johnson earned the fifth gold medal of his Olympic career to go with gold from the 1992 4x400 relay, 1996 200- and 400-meters and 2000 400-meters. Alvin Harrison (44.5) and Antonio Pettigrew (45.1) ran the first and second legs, respectively, building a lead of roughly two meters. Alvin's twin brother, Calvin, then built a cushion of several seconds on a leg timed in 43.6 seconds. Johnson (44.3) extended the lead and brought the relay home to finish in 2:56.35. Nigeria was second in 2:58.68 and Jamaica was third in 2:58.78.

"I feel great about my last victory," said Johnson. "There was a lot of pressure coming in here to end my Olympic career like I started it, winning gold. It's great to continue the reputation as the best men's 4x400 in the world."

And, with its performance at the 2000 Sydney Olympic Games, Team USA continued its reputation as the best track and field team in the world.

USA

51

Fans watch as players battle and shuttlecocks zoom across the nets during badminton competition in Olympic Pavilion.

BADMINTON

By Barb Kissick

Although overlooked in North America, badminton, a game that emphasizes agility and speed over power, is among the most popular sports in Japan, Indonesia and China where it has been played for 2,000 years. Shuttlecocks fly off rackets at speeds of up to 200 miles an hour before slowly floating to the ground, and are as popular in Asia as baseballs and footballs are in North America.

Until the 2000 Olympic Games in Sydney, the U.S. had never had a badminton athlete advance past the second round of play. Kevin Han, the United States' lone representative at the Games, was the only American athlete to qualify in men's singles

badminton competition. He received a bye in the round-of-64 to face Michael Beres of Canada whom he bested, 15-5 15-3. Han's next opponent was Xinpeng Ji of China, seeded seventh in the world. Han lost the match to Ji, who went on to win the gold medal. Nevertheless, Han made history as he became the first athlete from the Pan American region to advance to an Olympic round-of-16 match.

Before playing Xinpeng Ji, Han admitted, "I have nothing to lose," the age-old adage of underdogs. Kevin Han knows about life as an underdog, and he knows about struggling.

He was born in Shanghai, which is a good start for a badminton player. Asians nearly dominate the sport, winning 14 of 15 medals at the Atlanta Olympics. Kevin's mother encouraged him to try badminton at the age of 11, even though he preferred basketball. By the time he was 17, his parents were divorced and he came to the U.S. to live with his father. Kevin's home was a 2-bedroom apartment in Brooklyn, New York, where he worked as a busboy and delivery boy in a New York City Chinese restaurant.

Speaking no English made life even harder. Survival was the first order of business meaning sports took

a back seat. After a while, Kevin started playing badminton in New York clubs. He quickly attracted attention, which got him invited to train at the U.S. Olympic Education Center in Marquette, MI.

In 1994, Kevin became a U.S. citizen and also won the national badminton title. He moved to the Olympic Training Center in Colorado Springs, CO, started working, earned an associate degree from a community college and went on to earn an undergraduate degree in information technology from the University of Colorado at Colorado Springs. Kevin now works as a software engineer, is married and, of course, loves Asian foods and karaoke.

Kevin calls his 11 years in America, going from an immigrant restaurant worker to a national sports champion "an amazing ride."

Comprised of 16 feathers from left wing of a goose, the badminton shuttlecock flies across the net at speeds approaching 200 miles per hour making it nearly the fastest racket sport in the world.

Badminton competition was held at the Sydney Olympic Pavilion.

Al Bello/Allsport

BASEBALL

By Dave Fanucchi

As they say, baseball in America is like apple pie and Chevrolet. Every day, youngsters play the game all across our country's heartland. But until a legendary leader came along to guide Team USA into the Olympics, America had never touched gold in the sport they love so much.

For the first time in history, professional baseball players would be participating in the Olympic Games. That prompted USA Baseball to select a ragtag group of minor leaguers, to be led by Hall of Fame manager Tommy Lasorda. Their hopes: to dethrone two-time Olympic gold medalist, Cuba, and change the landscape of international baseball. "When these Olympic Games are over, I promise you that everybody in America will know your names," said Lasorda to his squad. "We're not going 6,000 miles to lose."

The Americans wasted no time. In their opening game against Japan, the score was tied 2-2 after nine innings. That was until an outfielder from Delaware named Mike Neill stepped to the plate in the bottom of the 13th inning. Neill blasted Japanese reliever Toshiya Sugiuchi's fastball high and deep over the fence in right field, lifting Team USA to a sudden victory.

"I've never felt so happy to see a ball go over the wall in my whole life," said the exuberant Neill.

Team USA then rattled off an 11-1 win over South Africa behind John Cotton's five RBIs, and 13 strikeouts in a complete-game effort from

Pitcher Ben Sheets falls to his knees in triumph as the U.S. defeats Cuba.

Kentucky right-hander Jon Rauch. They followed with a 6-2 triumph over the Netherlands, as both Brad Wilkerson and Ernie Young provided home runs. Team USA seemed well in control of both games, improving their record to 3-0.

That same team from the Netherlands delivered a major

shocker the next day: a 4-2 stunner over Cuba. It was Cuba's first-ever loss in Olympic competition, winning 21 straight games since 1992.

In Team USA's next match-up, the Koreans had the Red, White and Blue deadlocked in a scoreless game, as the sidearming Tae-Hyon Chong handcuffed the American bats all night. But USA pitcher Roy Oswalt matched zeros with Chong through seven innings until the Americans were able to load the bases in the bottom of the eighth. Doug Mientkiewicz strode to the plate with the game on the line.

"That's the situation my dad and I dreamed about when I was a kid," said the 26-year-old Minnesota Twins prospect. Mientkiewicz worked the count full off Korean reliever Pil-Jung Jin, and then turned on a fastball driving it into the night for a game-winning grand slam. "It was the greatest home run I've ever hit, certainly the most thrilling." Little did he know what was yet to come.

Lasorda's crew managed to coax a 4-2 win over Italy on their skipper's 73rd birthday. "This is the greatest gift I could ever ask for, a win over my father's homeland," said Lasorda. "It seems as though we always bring

54

Mike Neill is greeted by his teammates after hitting the homer that downed Japan.

Baseball icon Tommy Lasorda celebrates with his team after finishing off Korea in the semifinals.

out the best in every team we play. They all want to beat the United States." The win clinched a berth for Team USA in the Olympic medal round.

With the Americans standing as the only unbeaten team remaining, it was time to face their nemesis. Team USA went face-to-face with the Cubans for their only loss of the tournament, a bitter 6-1 defeat.

Team USA closed out pool play

with a 12-1 whitewashing of host country Australia. The Americans finished up the preliminary round robin with a 6-1 record.

In the semifinals, Team USA faced the stingy Koreans who had fought until the very end in their first meeting. Throughout a constant, light drizzle, Korea jumped out to an early 2-0 lead. Team USA battled back to bring the score even before the game was held for a gut-

wrenching two-hour rain delay. After play resumed, Mientkiewicz stepped up to end the wettest and wildest game in Olympic baseball history with a solo home run in the bottom of the ninth. The 3-2 semifinal win left the Americans deliriously jumping into each others' arms while the Miami native circled the bases, arms waving in joy. Mientkiewicz had had broken the Koreans' hearts for a second time.

Previous page:
Players celebrate in a sea of blue shirts piling onto the mound after crushing Cuba to take the gold medal.

Clockwise from top left:
Shane Heams pitches against Japan in the preliminary round.

Adam Everett turns a double play against Italy.

The U.S. team battles it out with Italy, giving Manager Tommy Lasorda a spot in the medal round as a 73rd birthday present.

Brent Abernathy makes a base hit against Australia.

Travis Dawkins (left) turns a double play as Brett Roneberg of Australia goes for second.

Next page:
Top: Manager Tommy Lasorda looks on as the U.S. takes down Japan in the preliminaries.

Bottom left: Ben Sheets pitches for six innings to help the U.S. conquer Italy.

Bottom right: The game against Japan was the longest ever played in Olympic history, going 13 innings until a home run from Mike Neill closed it out for the U.S.

Jed Jacobsohn/Allsport

Jamie Squire/Allsport

Jamie Squire/Allsport

Doug Pensinger/Allsport

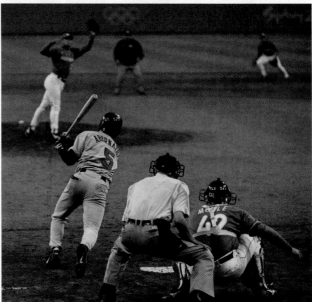

Doug Pensinger/Allsport

58

Jamie Squire/Allsport

Team USA had now set-up its rematch with Cuba for the gold medal. In a game that proved no contest, international baseball's dynasty went down with only three hits off the Louisiana Bayou's Ben Sheets, 4-0. Neill hit a first-inning homer to break the tension, while veteran Pat Borders added a run-scoring double and Young, a bases-loaded single. Those hits put the upset on the fingertips of Sheets, an unflappable right-hander who got 16 ground-ball outs in the first eight innings, setting up a pulsating ninth.

With the Americans standing on the front step of their dugout and an American flag hanging behind the bench, Sheets strode calmly to the mound. He got Cuba's first two hitters swinging, and when Neill made a sliding catch of Yasser

Travis Dawkins (left) and Reggie Smith have a word with an umpire during the semifinal against Korea.

The U.S. baseball team gathers to celebrate on the mound after defeating Cuba in the final game.

Adam Pretty/Allsport

Above: Team USA, decked out in Red, White, Blue and Gold, captures the moment.

Right: The U.S. team members are elated as they crush world baseball's superpower, Cuba, to bring the gold medal home where it belongs.

Gomez's fly in left field for the final out, Sheets fell to his knees and raised his arms in celebration as players streamed toward him for a huddle on the mound.

Soon, they piled up near the dirt at third base and their skipper, wearing a flag over his left shoulder, hugged his coaches while the players took a victory lap. "I've won World Series Championships before with the Dodgers," said the choked-up Lasorda, "but this is the greatest moment of my life."

The Cubans sat in their dugout stunned that their dynasty was done. The best team in international baseball had its hold on the gold broken by its biggest rival. The Olympic Gold medal in baseball was finally coming home.

USA

Vin Baker (left) and Kevin Garnett (right) battle Nikita Morgunov and Alexandre Bachminov of Russia for a rebound in the semifinal round.
At right: Vince Carter answers Lithuania with a winning basket to put the U.S. back on top with less than a minute to play.

BASKETBALL

USA ⚬⚬⚬⚬⚬

By Craig Miller (Men) and Caroline Williams (Women)

MEN

They did what they had come to do and what was expected: win the Olympic gold medal. What was not expected were several tight contests that kept the games suspenseful for U.S. team members and basketball fans worldwide.

The U.S. team opened play with an impressive 119-72 win over China, a team which featured the "Great Walking Wall," a frontline consisting of players who measured 7'5, 7'2 and 7'0. Italy, the 1999 European champions, fell two days later 93-61. The U.S. earned its third straight win by just nine points, 85-76, over the Lithuanian team which never let the U.S. break away. The next casualty of the U.S. streak, New Zealand, went

down to the U.S. 102-56. Closing out preliminary play, the U.S. improved to 5-0 after securing a 12-point win over France, 106-94

"This wasn't a day at the beach," said U.S. head coach Rudy Tomjanovich. "Just because we're from the United States, the other teams weren't going to just give up."

In the quarterfinals, the U.S. met its international rival, Russia, which kept things competitive for the first 20 minutes. Then the U.S. took control and posted an 85-70 win, the first U.S. Olympic win over a Russian or Soviet Union team since 1964.

In a semifinal rematch, Lithuania sent the U.S. a wake-up call when it proved its earlier nine-point loss was no fluke. In a game that saw the lead

change hands eight times in the second half, Lithuania gave the U.S. all it could handle as it rallied from a 12-point halftime deficit to take the game down to the wire.

Lithuania had taken an 81-80 lead with 41 seconds left in the game. Vince Carter and Antonio McDyess countered on the other end to give the lead back to the U.S., 84-81, with 0:24 remaining. Lithuania then cut the lead back to one, 84-83, with 10 seconds to go. On the U.S. inbounds pass, Jason Kidd was fouled and awarded a two free-throws. He made his first free-throw but missed the second, leaving the U.S. a 2-point lead. Then, after a scramble and a jump ball, and with four seconds showing on the clock, Lithuania was

awarded possession of the ball. Sarunas Jasikevicius, who scored 29 points and had nailed 5 of 10 three-pointers, rushed down court and launched a desperate three-pointer. Fortunately for the U.S., Jasikevicius' shot was well off target, cinching a tight 85-83 U.S. victory and giving the Americans a shot at France for the gold medal.

In another tight affair, holding a 16-point lead with 8:30 showing on the clock, the Americans were unable to put France away completely. France rallied to within four points, 76-72, with 4:26 to play before the U.S. reasserted itself and pulled away for the golden 85-75 victory.

The U.S.'s gold-medal-worthy team effort paid off. Offensively, the U.S. averaged 95.0 points a game and all 12 players scored between 5.5 and 14.8 points per game. Vince Carter, the team's youngest member at 23-years-old, led the U.S. in scoring and was third overall for the Games, averaging 14.8 points per game. Kevin Garnett added 10.8 points per game and a competition-leading 9.1 rebounds. Center Alonzo Mourning added 10.2 points per game, 4.2 rebounds and an Olympic high of 2.3 blocked shots per game. Ray Allen finished averaging 9.8 points per game and Jason Kidd led the U.S. and ranked fourth in the Games in assists averaging 4.4 per game. Two-time Olympian Gary Payton added 3.4 assists per game to rank eighth among all players.

Defensively, the U.S. limited its opponents to 73.4 points per game and just 39.0 percent shooting overall from the floor, including 28.1 percent from three-point range. The U.S. out-rebounded its opponents by 17.6 rebounds a game.

Lisa Leslie takes a jumper to put Cuba away in the preliminary round.

Sheryl Swoopes beats Patrycia Czepiec of Poland into the paint for a 76-57 victory.

Jamie Squire/Allsport

Katie Smith is alone under the basket for an easy lay-up.

Andy Lyons/Allsport

For the 12th time in 14 Olympic basketball competitions, the U.S. team won gold, and they did it without suffering a single loss. In fact, the Americans have now claimed victory in 109 of 111 Olympic basketball match-ups.

WOMEN

The 2000 U.S. women's Olympic basketball team rolled to an 8-0 record for the gold medal after defeating host and previously unbeaten Australia 76-54 in the final contest in Sydney. Defending its 1996 gold, the U.S. upped its overall Olympic record to 34-3 and has captured four gold medals (1984, 1988, 1996, 2000), one silver (1976) and one bronze (1992) in six Olympic outings.

USA National Team head mentor Nell Fortner closed her three-year USA Basketball career, leading the U.S. to perfect records and gold medals in international basketball's most important competitions: the Olympics and World Championship.

The U.S. won all five preliminary round games in convincing fashion, defeating South Korea 89-75, Cuba 90-51, Russia 88-77, New Zealand 93-42 and Poland 76-57.

Advancing as the top seed from Group B, the United States earned a 58-43 quarterfinal win over Slovakia, then dominated the second half to win the rematch against South Korea 78-65 in the medal semifinal.

Meeting the undefeated Australian

Above: U.S. head coach Nell Fortner closed her three years as head coach of U.S. Basketball's Women's Senior National Team with a 101-14 record.

At left: Natalie Williams goes for the rebound above teammate Lisa Leslie and Anna Kotocova of Slovakia.

Lower left: U.S. Men's Basketball Head Coach Rudy Tomjanovich looks on as his team battles France for the gold medal.

Below: Kevin Garnett shows Lithuania how it is done in the USA.

At right: Frederic Weis of France gets tangled up with Vince Carter as he goes for a dunk to eventually put France away 106-94 in pool play.

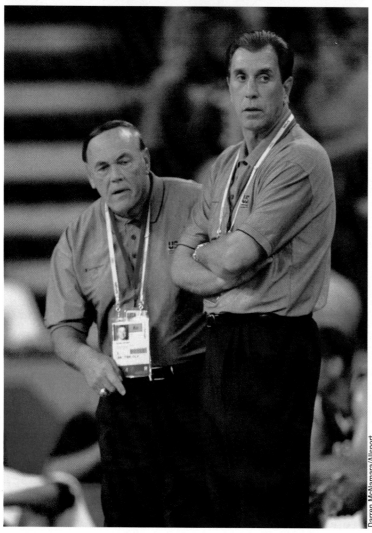

team in the gold medal game, the U.S. played its best game of the tournament to run away with a convincing 76-54 victory and the gold medal.

In the U.S.'s eight Olympic match-ups, the squad averaged 81.0 points a game while holding its opponents to 59.3 points. Relying on stifling defensive pressure, the Americans limited their opponents to 37.7 percent shooting from the floor, while its offense shot 50.8 percent. The U.S. also dominated on the boards, out-rebounding its foes by 14.7 rebounds per game.

Featuring a balanced offensive attack, the American effort was led by Lisa Leslie with 15.8 points per game, Sheryl Swoopes with 13.4 points per game and Yolanda Griffith added 11.5 points per game. Griffith led the squad on the glass averaging 8.8 rebounds per game while Leslie added 7.9 rebounds per game and Natalie Williams pulled in 5.9 rebounds per game. Team co-captains Dawn Staley and Teresa Edwards, along with Swoopes, dished out 3.6, 3.4 and 3.0 assists per game, respectively.

Swoopes commented, "This is a little better than 1996 for the simple fact that, at home, everybody expected us to win. But, everyone was saying Australia was going to beat us if they got here. That's what makes this sweeter."

The gold medal game marked the end of a brilliant 20-year career for Edwards who has played since 1981 on 22 different U.S. basketball teams. Edwards capped her career with an impressive grand total of 1,996 points and lists as the U.S.'s all-time Olympic career leader for games played (32), assists (143) and steals (59), and is second for points scored (265).

"I've had an impact on the game," said Edwards. "I think I've left a mark, etched something somewhere that people will remember me by when they talk about women's basketball. That's what you should strive to do in a career."

USA
🄾🄾🄾

At left: Australia's Michelle Griffiths is surrounded by U.S. defenders in the gold medal match-up.

Top: Vin Baker, Steve Smith, Tim Hardaway and Alonzo Mourning (left to right) watch anxiously as Lithuania gets dangerously close during the semifinal match.

Above: Antonio McDyess gets down on the ground and scrambles for the ball against France in the gold medal game.

Ricardo Williams (in red) goes up against eventual gold medalist for the Light Welterweight division Mahamadkadyz Abdullaev.

Below: Jose Navarro waits for the points decision over Hicham Mesbahi of Morocco.

BOXING

By Shilpa Bakre

The 2000 U.S. Olympic Boxing Team walked away from the Games without a gold medal for the first time since 1948, as both featherweight Ricardo Juarez of Houston, TX, and light welterweight Ricardo Williams, Jr., of Cincinnati, OH, fell short of winning their gold medal matches.

Although the final outcome was not as good as hoped for, there were several positives that will come from what is now being looked at as a learning experience.

"Obviously we feel like we could have done better," said Head Coach Tom Mustin. "But I think that we will be able to use this as motivation and a learning tool for 2004. There were several things that we did right, like educating our athletes about ringmanship and computerized scoring. We just barely hit the tip of the iceberg with international-style boxing. Now we need to continue to move forward."

Juarez faced an aggressive Bekzat Sattarkhanov of Kazakhstan. Unable to accomplish his game plan, Juarez was cautioned for holding at least nine times, although points were never taken. Despite a comeback in the third round, Juarez, who had fallen behind 15-4, was unable to take the victory.

"I am very disappointed," said Juarez. "I feel that the referee should have done more to control the fight." Gary Toney, Team Leader and President of USA Boxing filed a protest regarding the bout. As a result, the Russian referee was suspended for four years, however the decision in the bout was not overturned.

Williams faced an opponent who had defeated him at the World Championships. Mahamadkadyz Abdullaev of Uzbekistan, reigning World Champion, was looking for a gold medal while Williams came into the bout for revenge.

The first round was tentative for

70

Above: Ricardo Williams is declared the winner over Diogenes Luna Martinez of Cuba in the 63.5 kg division.

Left: Jermain Taylor (blue) defends himself against Yermakhan Ibraimov of Kazakhstan in the 71 kg semifinal.

Lower left: Ricardo Williams' good luck charm, his son Ricardo Williams III, takes him all the way to the silver medal.

Williams as he landed only one point with six seconds left. In the second round, action picked up but, unfortunately, it was on the side of Abdullaev. He was too strong for Williams which forced Williams be on the defensive. Williams tried to use his speed and movement to evade the Uzbek, but it was to no avail and he lost the bout 27-20. "I am proud of my performance and how far that I have come," said Williams.

Bamtamweight Clarence Vinson was able to secure one of the two bronze medals the team earned after a stunning performance against the reigning world champion. He received no break, however, as two days later he faced Cuban foe, Guillermo Rigondeaux Ortiz. Ortiz, at only 19 years of age and boxing in his first international tournament, showed he was among the best of the Cuban team. The southpaw proved to be too much for Vinson and defeated him 18-6.
"I am happy that I was able to come and at least get a medal, although I know that I am never happy. Had I gotten the gold I would have probably wanted platinum," said Vinson.

The other bronze medalist was light middleweight Jermain Taylor of Little Rock, AR. Taylor was facing 1996 bronze medalist Yermakahn Ibraimov of Kazakhstan. The southpaw gave Taylor trouble from the beginning and Taylor was never able to settle into his groove. Before he knew it, he was down by a considerable margin. He went on to lose the bout by a final score of 29-14.

"I just wasn't able to get off tonight," admitted Taylor. "I am disappointed in my performance and wish that I would have been able to start sooner. But it is too late for that now, and I am happy that I am able to walk away with at least a bronze medal. There are a lot of people here who are walking away with nothing."

USA OOOOO

Olanda Anderson (red) fights Rudolf Kraj of the Czech Republic.

Jeff Lacy (blue) knocks down Pawel Kakietek of Poland in the 75 kg division.

Brian Viloria (blue) takes on Brahim Asloum of France in a 48 kg bout.

Above: Jose Navarro (red) goes for Hermensen Ballo Ballo of Indonesia in the 51 kg weight class.

Left: Ricardo Williams (red) throws a right at Olusegun Ajose of Nigeria in the 63.5 kg division.

Lower left: Jermain Taylor (blue) dominates Dimitriy Usagin of Bulgaria for a first round victory in the 71 kg division.

Below: Ricardo Juarez (blue) gives a valiant effort before falling to Bekzat Sattarkhanov of Kazakhstan in the Featherweight division.

By Lisa Fish

The excitement of the Olympic Games began for USA Canoe/Kayak even before the cauldron was lit in Olympic Stadium to signify the opening of the 27th Olympiad.

For the first time in the Olympic Games history, a kayaker, Cliff Meidl of Redondo Beach, CA, was chosen unanimously by his peers to lead the U.S. delegation into Opening Ceremonies.

In 1986, Meidl was nearly killed while operating a jackhammer when he struck through three unmarked high-voltage cables. His body absorbed 30,000 volts of electricity and his knees came in direct contact with the jackhammer.

Meidl's legs were badly damaged and the shock caused other serious injuries. A radical procedure saved his legs from amputation and Meidl was determined to walk again. Inspired by 1988 kayak Olympian Greg Barton, another physically challenged athlete who earned two gold medals in Seoul, Korea, Meidl added paddling to his rehabilitation program. Meidl said, "I can't run or ski, but I can walk and I can paddle."

Another compelling saga was brewing for USA canoe/kayak when the Court of Arbitration for Sport rejected sprint kayaker Angel Perez's bid to represent the U.S. at the Olympic Games.

Cliff Meidl carries the flag and leads Team USA into the Sydney Olympic Stadium during the Opening Ceremonies.

Stu Foprster/Allsport

Stu Foprster/Allsport

Perez, now living in Miami, FL, had left Cuba in 1993. Having competed for Cuba in the 1992 Olympic Games, he fell under Rule 49 of the Olympic Charter. This rule requires that an athlete who changes nationality wait three years or have the permission of the former National Olympic Committee before representing a new country as an Olympian. Cuba refused to release Perez.

After two unsuccessful appeals, the U.S. Olympic Committee filed a final appeal to the International Court of Arbitration and Sport providing documentation that the U.S. Government has viewed Perez as a citizen longer than the three-year requirement. Four days later, the court ruled in Perez's favor.

Meidl, Perez and their teammates competed in nine of the twelve sprint medal events. Meidl and his partner Philippe Boccara, a six-time Olympian, paddled in the K-2 1000-meter race but did not advance to the finals.

Jordan Malloch of Seattle was the lone canoeist on the sprint team. He paddled in the C-1 500-meters and C-1 1000-meters, but did not advance past the heats.

Kathy Colin of Kailua, Hawaii and Tamara Jenkins of Seattle paddled the K-2 Whitewater 500-meters to a 6th place finish in the semifinals. Colin paddled the K-1 Whitewater 500-meters, also to a 6th place finish in semifinals.

Top: David Hearn navigates the course in the canoe singles whitewater slalom qualifying round.

Left: Rebecca Giddens paddles her way past the qualifying round and into the final women's kayak singles whitewater slalom competition.

Perez and Peter Newton of Bellevue, WA, qualified in the K-2 500-meter and in the K-4 1000-meter race, and were joined by Stein Jorgensen of San Diego and John Mooney of Eugene, Oregon, in the K-4 1000 meter race. The K-4 finished 6th in the finals, the highest finish ever for a U.S. boat in the K-4 and only the second time the U.S. has made the finals in that event.

On the last day of the 2000 Olympics, races were delayed for six hours by gale-force winds. The race began in even worse conditions, waves and whitecaps hammering the boats throughout the course. The Americans finished in 6th place in the worst weather they had ever raced in.

Five slalom paddlers competed in the Sydney Games. Former Olympians Scott Shipley of Poulsbo, WA, David Hearn of Bethesda, MD and Lecky Haller of Bryson City, NC, were joined by first-time Olympians Matt Taylor of Atlanta, GA, and Rebecca Giddens of Green Bay, WI. The U.S. finished with one 5th, one 7th and two 12th place finishes.

USA Canoe/Kayak left the 2000 Olympic Games without medals or victory celebrations, but with memories and pride which cannot be qualified by record books or medal counts, but rather by the impressions they leave in our minds and in our hearts.

USA
OOO

Top: Peter Newton and Angel Perez work together for a spot in the final in the men's K2 500-meter flatwater kayaking competition.

Center: Philippe Boccara and Cliff Meidl give their all in the men's K2 1000-meter kayak sprint.

Right: Stein Jorgensen, John Mooney, Peter Newton and Angel Perez paddle in the men's K4 1000-meter kayak sprint for a chance to compete in the final.

Robert Cianflone/Allsport

Shaun Botterill/Allsport

Above: Stein Jorgensen powers down the course to advance to the semifinal in the men's K1 500-meter kayak sprint.

Left: Scott Shipley maneuvers for a spot in the men's K1 kayak slalom final.

Bottom: A volunteer at the canoe and kayak finals holds onto his hat as high winds delay the races.

Darren England/Allsport

CYCLING

By Rich Wanninger

Derek Bouchard-Hall, Mariano Friedick, Erin Hartwell and Tommy Mulkey compete in the qualifying round of the men's Team Pursuit.

Nineteen of the 27-member U.S. Olympic cycling roster made their Olympic debut in Sydney. The veterans were among the most recognizable of the 600-plus U.S. athlete delegation - Lance Armstrong, Marty Nothstein and Chris Witty.

Aside from the gold (Nothstein), silver (Mari Holden) and bronze (Armstrong) medals, the Americans recorded 15 top-10 finishes, including Witty's fifth-place finish.

TRACK
Marty Nothstein's men's sprint medal in track cycling marked the first Olympic gold for the American cyclists since the 1984 Games.

In the semifinals, Nothstein, who took silver at the 1996 Games in Atlanta, defeated reigning Olympic gold medalist Jens Feidler of Germany in two races in the best two-of-three series. Nothstein defeated France's Florian Rousseau in two races to take the gold medal for the United States.

"I think of all the sacrifices me and my family have made...there have been a lot of tears, a lot of lost skin and a lot of sore muscles - tonight it made it all worth it," said Nothstein, winner of 22 national and three world titles.

Witty set an Olympic record when she posted her personal best time of 35.230 seconds. The two-time national 500-meter time trial champion was looking to become the first female U.S. Olympian and fourth Olympian overall to capture medals in the Summer and Winter Olympic Games.

Jame Carney made his second Olympic appearance in Sydney, placing fifth in the men's 40-kilometer points race. His was the highest U.S. finish in an Olympic points race since Frankie Andreu garnered eighth-place at the 1988 Olympic Games.

PERFORMANCE

Mike Powell/Allsport

Mike Powell/Allsport

"This race was for my dear friend Nicole Reinhart who was killed in a bicycle accident on September 17, 2000," said Carney. "I had her name on my helmet. She was a wonderful friend. Training without her won't be quite the same."

Among the other top-10 track performances were Nothstein (fifth, Keirin), Tanya Lindenmuth (sixth, match sprint), Erin Veenstra-Mirabella (eighth, individual pursuit; 10th, points race), Mariano Friedick (10th, individual pursuit) and the team pursuit squad of Friedick, Derek Bouchard-Hall, Tommy Mulkey and Erin Hartwell(10th).

ROAD
Lance Armstrong earned his first Olympic medal, a bronze, in the individual time trial. The winner of two consecutive Tour de France titles, Armstrong was considered a medal favorite throughout the race.

"I came to win the gold medal," said Armstrong. "When you prepare for an event, you come, and you do your best. I felt good, I went as hard as I could, and I got third."

Mari Holden gave a dramatic silver medal performance in the women's individual time trial. With her finish, the highlight of her career, she defeated cycling legend and holder of 11 world titles Jeannie Longo-Ciprelli of France for the first time.

"I focused the whole year on this race, so I am really excited that it actually worked out," said Holden. "I started out with such bad luck in the road race three days earlier. I had three wheel changes and a bike crash, so I was hoping for good luck today." After abandoning the road race due to the crash, Holden captured the first Olympic female road cycling medal for the United States since Connie-Carpenter-Phinney and Rebecca Twigg won the gold and silver medal at the

Above: Marty Nothstein shares a victory lap with his son, Tyler, after receiving the gold medal for men's sprint.

Previous page:
Top: Chris Witty rides to fifth place in the women's 500m time trial.
Bottom: "Tinker" Juarez speeds downhill in the men's cross country mountain bike race.

1984 Los Angeles Olympics in the road race.

Other top 10 road performances came from George Hincapie who finished eighth in the road race and Tyler Hamilton who came in 10th in individual time trials.

MOUNTAIN BIKE

Riding amidst the wombats, snakes and magpies, the American women were considered among the world's best competitors with three riders ranked among the top 15 in the world.

Alison Dunlap started in the first row and was standing second when her handlebars clipped a tree and she dropped to the ground. By the time she recovered, her chances for gold had vanished. Dunlap, the 1999 national champion, finished in seventh place. Ruthie Matthes and Ann Trombley placed 10th and 16th in their Olympic debut.

In the men's race, "Tinker" Juarez and Travis Brown were hampered by their starting positions in the fifth row and had difficulties moving among the leaders. Juarez jumped into the top 20 for part of the race, but the pace derailed most riders. Juarez finished 30th, while Brown placed 32nd.

USA

83

Above left and right: Jenny Keim prepares for and executes a dive in the women's 3-meter springboard competition.
Next page: Laura Wilkinson is on her way to a gold medal in the women's 10-meter platform diving final.

DIVING

By Seth Pederson

When she saw her coach running toward her, his arms outstretched and a wide smile on his face, Laura Wilkinson knew she had won. Against a field of Chinese top guns and upstart Canadians, Wilkinson's five-dive list on women's platform won the crowd and the judges alike in the 2000 Olympic Games' individual diving final.

It was an upset victory only the Olympic Games can produce. Wilkinson, 22, entered the final seeded fifth behind favorites like Li Na of China, the 2000 FINA World Cup gold medalist; Sang Xue of China, the 1999 FINA World Cup gold medalist; and Emilie Heymans of Canada, who boasted the most difficult list of the contest.

No one ever said that Olympic competition would be easy, and jumping into gold-medal contention from fifth place is a difficult task in any contest. Wilkinson stayed locked there after the first two rounds, even though her armstand back double somersault with $\frac{1}{2}$ twist pike and back 2 $\frac{1}{2}$ somersaults pike dives earned 8.0s and 8.5s from the judges.

The 8.0s and 9.0s awarded to Li, Heymans and Anne Montminy of Canada in those rounds kept Laura from moving up the ladder.

But Wilkinson's third round reverse 2 $\frac{1}{2}$ somersault tuck turned the contest around. For the same dive that earned her six 10.0s at the U.S. Olympic Trials in June and five 10.0s at the U.S. Outdoor Nationals in August, Wilkinson won 9.0s and 9.5s and jumped into first by one point. And she never let go.

Wilkinson performed her last two dives virtually flawlessly, accepting

nothing less than an 8.0 on her inward 2 ½ somersault pike and back 2 ½ somersault with ½ twist pike.

The results amazed everyone, but no one was too surprised. "She worked hard," said teammate Troy Dumais, who competed later in both the individual and synchronized men's 3-meter events. "She's been through some big road blocks and busted through them. She showed the United States that anything is possible."

Wilkinson's platform success marked the end of a 36-year gold-medal drought on the board for the U.S. and incited the other American divers to live up to her achievement. But traditional powerhouses like China and Russia, alongside Mexico, Canada and even Australia, had other ideas and shut out Team USA's best hopes for additional individual medals. In the end, they walked away with the lion's share of medals, even stockpiling most from the newest addition to Olympic diving, synchronized diving. Troy Dumais, Mark Ruiz, David Pichler, Michelle Davison, Jenny Keim and Sara Reiling each faced a wall of international competition too great to overcome.

Marking the first time the Olympic diving schedule had grown since 1920, four synchronized diving events were added for the 2000 Games. Although the U.S. was able to take home medals in synchronized events at international meets leading up to the Games, U.S. pairs were unable to live up to that expectation on men's synchro 3-meter and platform and women' synchro platform.

The final tally was one fabulous gold medal sparkling on the neck of Texas' newest champion, Laura Wilkinson. Her enthusiasm and genuine excitement after the big win not only made the country cheer, but gave the entire diving team a proud moment of glory.

Top left and right: Mark Ruiz executes a reverse dive in the pike position.
Center: Michelle Davison Competes in the women's 3-meter springboard.
Bottom left and right: Troy Dumais competes in men's 3-meter springboard and 10-meter platform.

USA

Laura Wilkinson (left) and Jenny Keim are in-synch for a fifth place finish in the first women's pairs synchronized 10-meter platform final.

Scott Barbour/Allsport

EQUESTRIAN

USA

By Marty Bauman

David O'Connor of The Plains, VA, won the first Olympic gold medal for the U.S. Equestrian Team since 1984 when he clinched the Individual Eventing gold on Custom Made, a 15-year-old Irish Thoroughbred gelding owned by Xandarius, LLC.

O'Connor's performance topped an excellent Olympic showing for the U.S. which included a pair of team bronze medals, one in Eventing and one in Dressage.

O'Connor finished the three-phase Eventing competition with a score of 34.00 penalties, the best score in Olympic history. Placing second was Andrew Hoy of Australia with a score of 39.80 on Swizzle In and two-time Olympic champion Mark Todd of New Zealand was third with a score of 42.00 on Eye Spy II.

In Individual Eventing, Bobby Costello of Southern Pines, NC, finished eighth on Chevalier, an 11-year-old Thoroughbred gelding owned by Deirdre Pirie, and Julie Black of Newnan, GA, finished ninth on Hyde Park Corner, a 10-year-old American Thoroughbred gelding owned by Jim and Janet Richards.

In Team Eventing, the U.S. won the bronze medal with a three-phase total of 175.80 penalties. Australia won the team gold for the third consecutive time and Great Britain won the silver.

O'Connor turned in one of only three fault-free rides in the final jumping phase on Giltedge, a 14-year-old Irish Thoroughbred gelding owned by Jacqueline Mars. Joining O'Connor on the team was his wife,

Above: David O'Connor rides Custom Made in Individual Three-Day Event Show Jumping.

At right: Margie Goldstein Engle rides Perin to a 10th place finish in Individual Jumping.

David O'Connor and Giltedge give a fault-free performance in the final jumping phase of the Three-Day Event Show Jumping competition to take the bronze medal.

Robert Costello takes Chevalier through a water jump for an eighth place finish in Individual Eventing.

Al Bello/Allsport

Darren McNamara/Allsport

David O'Connor takes Custom Made into the water on their way to the gold medal in Individual Eventing.

best score ever (1,746 points, 69.84%) and gave the U.S. its third consecutive Olympic team bronze medal in dressage.

Joining Traurig and Seidel on the medal stand was Sue Blinks of Wellington, FL, who scored 69.00% (1725 points) on Flim Flam, a 13-year-old Hanoverian gelding owned by Fritz Kundrun and the Dressage Sponsor Corporation. Team captain Robert Dover of Flemington, NJ, in his fifth Olympic Games, more than any other U.S. dressage rider, started the U.S. off with a score of 1678 (67.12%) on Ranier, a 9-year-old Oldenburg gelding owned by Jane Clark. Guenter Seidel of Del Mar, CA, scored 1695 points (61.80%) on Dick and Jane Brown's Foltaire.

In Individual Dressage, Blinks finished eighth, while Traurig wound up 11th.

The gold medal went to Anky van Grunsven of The Netherlands on Bonfire, with silver going to defending Olympic champion Isabell Werth of Germany on Gigolo, and bronze going to another German, Ulla Salzgeber.

After the first round of Team Show Jumping, Germany, France and Switzerland each had 8 faults to tie for first, making it a close and exciting race for the medals. Germany pulled away in the second round and won the gold with a total of 15 penalties. Its closest rival, Switzerland, won the silver with 16 penalties. Brazil took bronze after a jump-off with France. After being in contention for the team bronze in the first round, U.S. riders faded during the second round, landing in sixth-place.

Individually, Marie Engle of Wellington, FL, was the top finisher, ending in a tie for 10th. Lauren Hough of Ocala, FL, wound up tied for 15th.

Jeroen Dubbeldam and Albert Voorn of The Netherlands won gold and silver while Khaled Al Eid of Saudi Arabia won bronze.

Karen, on Prince Panache, a 16-year-old British Thoroughbred gelding owned by Jacqueline Mars; Nina Fout of Middleburg, VA, on her 3 Magic Beans, a 10-year-old American Thoroughbred gelding; and Linden Wiesman of Bluemont, VA, on

Anderoo, an 11-year-old American Thoroughbred gelding owned by James and Barbara Wiesman.

In Dressage, Christine Traurig of Carlsbad, CA, rode Etienne, a 12-year-old Westphalian gelding owned by Mr. and Mrs. Robert Haas, to his

FENCING

By Bill Hancock

Tamir Bloom faces Arnd Schmitt of Germany in Round 2 of the men's Individual Épée.

Stu Forster /Allsport

The fencing team recorded one of the United States' best performances in fencing in Olympic history at the Sydney Games. While the U.S. did not win any medals, the team performed well and showed the world that the United States will be a force in world fencing in the future.

The U.S. women's foil team earned its first Olympic medal-round appearance with a 45-41 upset victory over Hungary in the quarterfinals. The American team, Ann Marsh of Rochester, NY, and sisters Iris and Felicia Zimmerman of Rush, NY-lost in thrilling fashion to Germany, 45-42, in a bronze medal

bout that ended on an unusual note. Marsh was penalized for covering her target on the last touch by Germany's Rita Koenig. The penalty, the second against Marsh during the bout, gave Germany the winning point.

The U.S. women finished fourth, the best U.S. finish in Olympic history.

In women's individual foil, Iris Zimmerman finished 11th, Marsh finished 16th and Felicia Zimmerman finished 20th. Arlene Stevens of Fresh Meadows, NY, advanced to the second round of the women's épée competition before losing to Ildiko Mincza of Hungary.

Cliff Bayer of New York City recorded the top American individual finish. His 10th place was the best finish by an American men's fencer since 1984. Bayer took the eventual champion to the wire, leading his bout with Young-Ho Kim of Korea 11-7, 13-10 and finally 14-13 before the Korean saved the match by taking the final two touches to win 15-14.

"Kim is one of the best guys out there," said Bayer. "I really feel like I fenced well." Bayer had reached the round of 16 by turning in an excellent performance in the second half of his bout with Ryszard Sobczak of Poland. Trailing 8-6,

Above: Iris Zimmermann (right) takes on Volga Charkova of Russia in the women's Individual Foil.

Below: Women's Individual Foil fencers meet in competition at the Sydney Convention and Exhibition Center in Darling Harbor

Bayer scored nine of the final 10 touches in the bout to win, 15-9.

Keeth Smart of Brooklyn, NY, reached the second round of the men's saber competition and eventually finished 30th. His countryman, Akhi Spencer-El of New York City, lost his first-round bout and finished 34th.

In men's épée, American Tamir Bloom reached the second round where, after battling back from a 6-1 deficit, he lost 15-12 to World Champion Arnd Schmitt of Germany.

"I'm very proud of these athletes," said USA Fencing executive director Michael Massik. "We have come a long way in fencing in the United States."

GYMNASTICS

By Susan Polakoff Shaw

WOMEN'S TEAM

Although they were unable to repeat their golden performance of the Atlanta Games, the U.S. women's gymnastics team finished in fourth place, a pleasing result for a unique team.

A combination of Olympic medallists, Dominque Dawes and Amy Chow, World Championship team members Elise Ray, Jamie Dantzscher, and Kristen Maloney and youth Tasha Schwikert pulled together after a shaky start in the team preliminaries. The team finished the round in a disappointing sixth place suffering falls, boundary violations and generally delivering an uninspired performance, but managed to advance to the finals where the U.S. showed spirit and focus. Marching into the Sydney SuperDome waving small American flags, the team appeared to have regrouped.

The evening's top performance came when Chow scored a 9.70 on the uneven bars. The 1996 silver medallist finished in 16th place overall. Maloney turned in the team's highest floor mark, a 9.737. The U.S. team finished second on bars, third on floor, fifth on vault and sixth on beam.

Romania claimed the team gold medal. Russia was second and China finished third.

WOMEN'S ALL-AROUND

Led by Andrea Raducan, Romania swept the women's all-around competition for the first time, but faulty equipment and the first positive drug test in Olympic gymnastics history became the real story.

During the competition, it was discovered that the vault horse was set five centimeters too low, resulting in numerous falls and low vault scores during the first and second rotations.

With vault as her first event, national champion Elise Ray fell victim to the improper setting, landing on her back during warm-up and falling on both vaults. "I didn't know what was wrong," said Ray. "Falling on your first event out definitely shoots your confidence." Ray scored 9.750 on bars, but fell off

Above: Amy Chow flies through the air in her floor exercise.

Next page:
Top: Morgan Hamm performs his floor exercise in the team finals. Bottom left: Paul Hamm vaults to third place in the team final competition. Bottom right: Blaine Wilson performs on the high bar for a 9.525 in the individual all-around.

Gary M. Prior/Allsport

beam scoring an 8.887. She recorded a 9.537 on floor.

Gymnasts from the first and second rotations were allowed to vault over in an unprecedented fifth rotation. Ray scored a 9.487. As the top American finisher at the 1999 World Championships, Ray was the United States' best hope at an all-around medal. After her score was adjusted, Ray finished 14th. Amy Chow was 15th and Kristen Maloney finished 20th.

Andrea Raducan became the first Romanian since Nadia Comaneci to win an Olympic all-around title. But, in an unusual turn of events, she was stripped of her gold medal after testing positive for pseudoephedrine, a banned substance found in common cold medication.

The gold was then awarded to Simona Amanar of Romania; Romanian teammate Maria Olaru received the silver and Liu Xuan of China who had finished fourth claimed the bronze. Raducan was allowed to keep her gold medal from the team competition and silver from the individual vault. This was the first positive drug test in Olympic gymnastics.

TRAMPOLINE

Irina Karavaeva of Russia took the gold medal at the first Olympic trampoline competition. Oxana Tsyhuleva of Ukraine won the silver and Karen Cockburn of Canada won the bronze. Each of the 12 gymnasts competed a compulsory and optional routine. The top eight gymnasts went on to perform a single optional routine.

Finishing the preliminary round in ninth place, American Jennifer Parilla of Lake Forrest, CA, failed to advance to the finals

"I am 19 and the youngest trampolinist here," said Parilla. "We've got a lot of world champions here with more experience, but I will be back in 2004 and I will be more in my prime then. I will be

Above: Amy Chow vaults in the women's team competition.

At right: Kristen Maloney scores a 9.537 for her beam exercise in the team final.

Below: Women's team competition takes place at the Sydney Superdome.

Next page: Blaine Wilson achieves his best score on the parallel bars in the men's team final.

around for awhile."

Inventor of the trampoline, American George Nissen, now 86, was on hand to watch the historic competition.

MEN'S TEAM

In team preliminaries, the U.S. men rallied in the final rotations to finish in fourth place and advanced to the finals. Medal hopes for the men's team fell short as the squad settled for a fifth place finish in the finals.

"I thought we could have won a medal, for sure," said Peter Kormann, men's team Olympic coach. "We had some mistakes on most events and, in a meet like this, you just can't have that."

China dominated the team competition to claim gold. Ukraine was second with Russia third. Blaine Wilson finished in eighth place overall, having fallen off high bar and stepping out of bounds on floor. His best score, 9.775, came on parallel bars. Paul Hamm finished 13th overall.

"He (Blaine) helped us get into the finals, which is all we asked him to do," said Kormann. "Blaine Wilson being perfect tonight would not have been enough for our team to win a medal."

Steve McCain re-injured his right ankle on vault, but hung on to perform on parallel bars and high bar. "I'm not too disappointed," said McCain. "No one gave up and everybody fought hard out there. It's a little heartbreaking for someone like myself, because this might be my last competition."

The buzz from the men's meet was created by 17-year-old twin sensations Morgan and Paul Hamm of Waukesha, WI. The brothers turned in solid performances throughout most of the competition and celebrated their 18th birthdays during the Games.

Three-time Olympian John Roethlisberger, 30, dislocated his finger during touch warm-ups in

Above: The U.S. men's team prepares.

At left: Sean Townsend vaults in the team final.

pommel horse, but still managed to score a 9.60. On high bar, he nearly fell but dramatically re-grasped the bar with one hand and scored a 9.187.

Out of the six teams performing during the team finals, the U.S. finished first on parallel bars but fifth on every other event.

MEN'S ALL-AROUND

Five-time U.S. national all-around champion Blaine Wilson finished the all-around competition in sixth place, just 0.088 point away from a bronze medal. Steve McCain withdrew from the all-around due to an ankle injury sustained in the team finals. Hamm was a little shaken when he slipped off the high bar, his first event, but scored well on his remaining events.

Alexi Nemov of Russia, the 1996 Olympic silver medallist, won the all-around title. Wei Yang of China took silver and Aleksander Beresh of Ukraine, the 2000 European all-around champion, took bronze.

"This is all about learning to deal with the pressure," said Hamm. Five-time national champion, Blaine Wilson, is encouraged by his young teammates. "Look at Paul Hamm," said Wilson. "Give that kid a couple of years and he will beat gymnasts like Nemov; he's got that style. "

EVENT FINALS

Blaine Wilson finished sixth in the event finals for vault, Elise Ray was eighth on beam and on his 18th birthday, Morgan Hamm, finished the floor exercise event final in seventh place.

This is the first time since 1972 that the U.S. has not collected a medal in Olympic gymnastics.

"We knew this was going to be tough coming in, but we thought we would be better than we were here," Bob Colarossi, USA Gymnastics President said. "The planning for Athens starts tomorrow."

USA

Brandan Greczkowski won three of his five match-ups in the 60 kg weight class.

JUDO

By Gary Abbott

The U.S. Olympic judo team went through many ups and downs during the 2000 Olympic Games. The highs were exhilarating and the lows were devastating as many athletes fell just short of clenching a medal. It was seven days of emotional competition, and the U.S. team was feeling the excitement.

The team qualified participants in all seven weight classes for the men's and women's tournament, one of the few teams to qualify a full squad. While the team began with medal hopes, the U.S. finished with a fifth place, two seventh place finishes and a number of outstanding performances. For some of the team members, the 2000 Olympic Games marked their best individual efforts on the world stage to date.

The 1999 World Champion at 73 kg (160 lbs.) and the most decorated judoka in American history, Jimmy Pedro of Lawrence, MA, turned in the top performance. The U.S. had won 10 previous judo medals, none of them gold, and Pedro was hoping to close his career with a historic day of competition. But, his hopes were crushed when he was defeated in his opening bout by Yong-Sin Choi of Korea.

Pedro made a valiant run at the bronze medal, winning four straight matches and progressing to the bronze medal round. In that match, Anatoly Laryukov of Belarus threw Pedro for an *ippon*, an instant victory, just 31 seconds into the match. The loss placed Pedro fifth in the division.

Brandan Greczkowski of Colorado Springs, CO, at 60 kg (132 lbs.), and Brian Olson of Colorado Springs, CO, at 90 kg (198 lbs.), put together strong efforts to place seventh, falling one match short of qualifying for the

Action takes place during the men's 90 kg Judo event at the Sydney Convention and Exhibition Centre in Darling Harbour.

bronze medal bout. It was the top international finish for Greczkowski who was competing in his first Olympic Games.

Three U.S. athletes completed the tournament with 2-2 records, falling just short of making the medal round: Celita Schutz, Hillsdale, NJ, in the women's 63 kg (139 lbs.) division, Colleen Rosensteel, Buffalo Grove, IL, in the +78 kg (172 lbs.) division and Ato Hand, Colorado Springs, CO, in

the men's 100 kg (220 lbs.) division. These were, in effect, ninth place finishes.

Other U.S. men's team members were Alex Ottiano of Lawrence, MA, at 66 kg (145 lbs.) with a 1-1 record, Jason Morris of Scotia, NY, at 81 kg (178 lbs.) with an 0-1 record, and Martin Boonzaayer of Palatine, IL, with an 0-1 record. Morris, a four-time Olympian and former Olympic silver medalist, was injured early in his first match and

lost a close decision.

Other U.S. women's team members were Lauren Meece of Pembroke Pines, FL, at 48 kg (106 lbs.) with a 0-1 record, Hillary Wolf of Chicago, IL, at 52 kg (115 lbs.) with a 0-2 record, Ellen Wilson of Colorado Springs, CO, with a 0-2 record, Sandra Bacher of San Jose, CA, with a 1-2 record and Amy Tong of San Jose, CA, with a 1-2 record.

Emily deRiel takes the Riding round and ends up on the silver medal.

MODERN PENTATHLON USA

By Bill Hancock

For the United States modern pentathlon Olympians, the evaluation of the results in Sydney was simple: it was the best U.S. performance in Olympic history.

Emily deRiel of Havertown, PA, claimed a silver medal for the United States in the first Olympic women's modern pentathlon competition. DeRiel's teammate, Mary Beth Iagorashvili, finished fourth.

In the men's event, two U.S. athletes finished in the top ten for the first time ever: Chad Senior of

Ft. Myers, FL, finished sixth and Velizar Iliev of San Antonio, TX, ninth.

deRiel was in first place going into the final event, a 3,000-meter run. As leader, under the unique modern pentathlon format, she began the run with a head start over the other competitors. England's Stephanie Cook overcame a 49 second gap to overtake deRiel in the last 300 meters and claim the gold medal.

"I feel great," said the 26-year-old

deRiel. "It wasn't disappointing to finish second. I'm very proud to have won an Olympic medal!"

Olympic women's modern pentathlon encompassed a shooting competition followed by round-robin fencing competition among all 24 competitors, a 200-meter freestyle swim, a 12-jump equestrian event and a three-kilometer run.

In the men's event, Senior was in first place after three events. The 25-year-old finished second in fencing and second in swimming to grab the

Mary Beth Iagorashvili cruises to a fourth place finish in the women's modern pentathlon.

Chad Senior, the medal favorite for the U.S., has trouble with his horse and falls to sixth place.

lead entering the riding event. But penalties for three refusals and two knockdowns on his horse, Riverina, left him in ninth place entering the three-kilometer run. He improved to sixth, but no higher.

"The horse just got away from me and I couldn't get him back," Senior said. "To me, that horse's name was 'Heartbreak'."

After four events, Iliev was leading. A strong ride vaulted him from seventh place into a tie for first. In the last event, the run, he took a 40-yard lead early in the race, but he faltered at the end as his legs began to cramp.

"We can look back with pride on this performance," said team leader Jim Gregory. "Overall, it was a

wonderful two days for our team, and for the sport of modern pentathlon."

Crowds of more than 14,000 witnessed the riding and running events each day in Sydney Olympic Park's baseball stadium. Spectators were even on hand for the 6:45 a.m. shooting competition.

ROWING

USA ⭕⭕⭕

By Brett Johnson

United States rowers qualified in nine of 14 finals and came home with three medals from the 2000 Olympic Games. The men's pair captured the silver medal and the women's pair and the women's lightweight double sculls won bronze medals.

Only two weeks before of the Games, the men's pair tandem of Sebastian Bea and Ted Murphy was not sure it would be able to compete. In July, Bea suffered a back injury and when he arrived in Sydney in late August, his back went into spasms again. Bea spent the first week of the team's two-week training camp lying

Top: Ted Murphy (left) and Sebastian Bea row in the coxless pair semifinals and advance to an eventual silver medal.

Right: The sun rises over an early morning practice session at the Sydney International Regatta Center at Penrith.

Top: Raj Shah, Katie Maloney, Linda Miller, Amy Martin, Betsy McCagg, Torrey Folk, Amy Fuller, Sarah Jones and Lianne Nelson advance to the final round of the women's eight.

Middle: Ruth Davidon (left) and Carol Skricki battle it out with Lithuania in the double sculls repechage.

Bottom: Karen Kraft (left) and Missy Ryan row to second place in their heat in the coxless pair.

Above: The U.S. men advance to the finals in the men's eight. Below: U.S. coxless four take second in their heat to advance to the semifinal.

Steve Tucker (left) and Conal Groom progress to the finals in lightweight double sculls.

on the floor of his condominium and only resumed rowing two weeks before the Games. The duo steadily progressed throughout the competition and, put together an outstanding race in the final, finishing less than one second behind the gold-medal-winning French. Both Murphy and Bea credited Kurt Borcherding, an alternate on the Olympic squad who rowed in place of Bea while he was injured. Bea and Murphy even placed Kurt's name on their boat, a tradition in rowing.

The women's pair of Karen Kraft and Missy (Schwen) Ryan claimed U.S. Rowing's first medal of the Games, a bronze. In 1996, Kraft and Ryan missed the top prize by 0.39 seconds. After taking two years off,

the duo decided to try it again. Their comeback was riddled with setbacks, including a lack of funding and a loss at the 1999 U.S. Rowing World Championship Trials. But, a victory at the 2000 Olympic Team Trials gave them an Olympic opportunity. In the final, Kraft and Ryan raced their game plan to perfection, getting out fast and leading until the 1,500-meter mark. However, the Romanian and Australian crews edged out the U.S. pair in the last 500 meters.

The women's lightweight double sculls tandem of Sarah Garner and Christine Collins rounded out the U.S. medalists. The duo claimed a bronze medal on the final day of competition. Like the women's pair, Garner and Collins took an early lead

and were in position to see when the other crews made their moves. Romania and Germany were able to row through the U.S. duo in the third quarter of the race to take the top two spots. The bronze medal gave Garner and Collins three medals, one Olympic and two world championships, in three years in the event.

Unfortunately for the U.S., the Olympic regatta was marked by disappointment as well. Although nine crews made the finals, including every sweep boat, the three-time defending world champion men's eight and two-time defending world silver medalist women's eight fell short of the medal stand.

SAILING

By Barby MacGowan

Star-class World Champions Mark Reynolds and Magnus Liljedahl are on their way to becoming Olympic Champions.

Considering an average age of 36, the 2000 Olympic Sailing Team was one of the oldest teams ever fielded by the U.S. It was also one of the most formidable teams in terms of experience.

Of the 18 sailors, 11 were repeating Olympians and eight of those were medalists. The Star and Soling teams were current world champions in their classes and the 470 men's team had recently soared to number one in world rankings.

Even the team's first-time Olympians were well-seasoned competitors. All this talent combined with the spectacular venue of Rushcutters Bay and a field of play of Sydney Harbor and the Tasman Sea off Sydney Heads was a recipe for success.

Out of the 69 countries competing, the U.S. was one of the six that qualified in all of the 11 sailing disciplines. The Americans proved their worthiness by bringing home four medals: one gold, two

silvers and a bronze. While Australia matched the record, only Great Britain, which claimed five medals, topped it.

An intense, staggered racing schedule spanned 14 days and accommodated 402 sailors. The debut of a 16-foot, high-performance skiff called the 49er highlighted the first half of the program. With its double trapeze, retractable wings and super-size sail area, the 49er blazed its way into the hearts of thousands

Top: Paul Foerster and Bob Merrick have a good lead on the rest of the fleet in men's 470 fleet races.

Above: JJ Eisler and Pease Glaser battle rough waters to take the silver medal in women's 470.

of sailing fans cheering from spectator boats and headlands.

It was two previous Olympic medalists, Seattle's sibling team of Jonathan and Charlie McKee, who won the first bronze medal in the new class. Jonathan represented the U.S. 16 years earlier to win the 1984 Flying Dutchman gold medal. In 1988, Charlie crewed to win the 470 men's bronze. Performing with critical precision, the McKee brothers conceded only to Finland and Great Britain.

The McKees were the only U.S. team on the podium for the first medal ceremony marking the conclusion of Tornado and Mistral men's and women's racing. The regatta was plagued by weak, fickle winds that took their toll on many teams, including the Tornado-class team of John Lovell and Charlie Ogletree. The duo settled for seventh in the end.

Boardsailing veterans Lanee Butler and Mike Gebhardt could not turn the light-air odds in their favor, either. Butler, however, finished a commendably solid fourth out of 29 entrants, while Gebhardt finished 11th out of 36 in their respective Mistral events.

For the second half of competition, the wind picked up but still imposed stiff challenges on the racecourses. One day there were geographical influences of nearby bluffs; the next, there were ocean swells so high the marks were barely visible. Nevertheless, the second medal ceremony bore more fruit for the U.S. with the 470 men's and women's teams claiming silver medals and the Star team taking gold.

Going home without a medal was especially difficult for Soling World Champions Jeff Madrigali, Craig Healy and Hartwell Jordan. With skipper Madrigali as a returning bronze medalist, the team had been one of the favored going in, but finishing fourth among 16 teams in fleet racing, the threesome was eliminated from further competition.

In the Europe class, 1996 bronze medalist Courtenay Dey finished 16th, while Finn sailor Russ Silvestri finished sixth.

It was a different story for 470 Women's Division sailor, JJ Isler and her crew Pease Glaser. An intuitive decision to take a hitch into the headlands during the final leg of their last harbor course race propelled them from a no-show position to a silver-medal-winning one. Snagging the gold was Australia with Ukraine taking the bronze.

In the 470 men's division, skipper Paul Foerster and crew Bob Merrick never gave any reason to doubt their ability to win a medal. It was only a matter of color, and that was decided in the last race of the 11-race series. The U.S. men sailed to a silver medal while Australia won the gold and Argentina took the bronze.

In one of the greatest comebacks in Olympic sailing history, 2000 Star World Champions Mark Reynolds and Magnus Liljedahl captured the gold medal on the final day of the Sydney Olympic Regatta. Assured of at least a bronze, the duo had to battle Brazil and Great Britain in their bid for a better medal color.

The drama of the final race beat all the rest. After an hour's weather delay, the shifty, difficult to read wind was blowing 10-12 knots. Brazil's aggressive tactics at the start backfired when they jumped the gun. Brazil never turned back which disqualified them and stripped them of their golden opportunity. Reynolds and Liljedahl also crossed the start early, but immediately spun around the pin to exonerate themselves.

Previous page: J.J. Isler and Pease Glaser enjoy a spectacular view during the 470 fleet races.

Top: Brothers Jonathan and Charlie McKee hike out in fleet races for the newly created class, the 49er.

Middle: Thomas Johanson and Jyrki Jarvi of Finland, Ian Barker and Simon Hiscocks of Great Britain and the McKee brothers sail to overall gold, overall silver and 49er bronze medals.

Right: John Myrdal sails to a 12th place finish in the Laser class.

Top: In the Soling fleet race, the team of Jeff Madrigali, Craig Healy and Hartwell Jordan fend off the Australian pursuit.

Bottom left and right: Lanee Butler and Mike Gebhardt sail to fourth and 12th place finishes in women's and men's Mistral.

Above: Tornado sailors battle for position at the start.

Bottom right: Paul Foerster and Bob Merrick head downwind for the 470-class gold medal.

Below: John Lovell and Charlie Ogletree fell victim to light, shifty winds in Tornado competition.

Bottom left: U.S. 470-class silver medalists Paul Foerster and Bob Merrick congratulate the Australian gold medalists Mark Turnbull and Tom King.

Above: U.S. Europe-class sailor Courtenay Dey sails by one of the most beautiful backdrops in the world, Sydney Harbor.

Below:Mike Gebhardt passes a mark in the Mistral fleet races on his way to an 11th place finish.

"The U.S. restarted, ducked several transoms and went right, as did Canada, while everyone else went left," said Team Leader Hal Haenel. "Then Canada rounded the top mark in first, and the U.S. was right behind them. It was a beautiful thing."

Reynolds and Liljedahl held their second-place position not knowing that Brazil was out of gold contention. In the end, the U.S. stole the gold, Great Britain maintained for silver and Brazil salvaged the bronze despite their blunder. Reynolds at 44 and Liljedahl at 46, the oldest athletes on the team, proved themselves for the second time in the same year as the very best Star sailors in the world.

Hamish Blair/Allsport

SHOOTING

USA

By Tori Svenningson

The American shooting team repeated its three-medal success of the 1996 Olympic Games when it brought home three more medals from Sydney: a gold in women's air rifle and two bronzes in women's double trap and men's skeet.

Shooting star Nancy Johnson had the golden touch when she shot right into the spotlight as the first medalist of the 2000 Olympic Games in Sydney.

"I had no idea I had medaled but when I saw my husband [fellow Olympian Ken Johnson] and father jumping up and down, I knew what color I had," she said following the match.

Cho-Hyun Kang of Korea won the silver medal, and Jing Gao of China won bronze.

The next American win went to Kim Rhode, who claimed her second Olympic medal by walking away

with the bronze in women's double trap. The 1996 gold medalist remains as awed as ever by the spectacle of the Olympic Games.

"This Olympics is a totally separate

Hamish Blair/Allsport

Top: Nancy Johnson takes aim at the gold medal in women's 10m air rifle. Above: Johnson knows what color medal she will be taking home.

event for me than the last one, but it's still amazing. It's just an incredible experience," said Rhode. Sweden's Pia Hansen captured the gold for her country, while Deborah Gelisio of Italy claimed the silver medal.

In a fitting response to an Olympics that had begun with an American medal, Todd Graves wrapped up the Games with a bronze medal of his own. A veteran of the 1992 and 1996 Olympic Games, the Mississippi native discovered the third time was just the magic he needed to secure his status as an Olympic medal winner. "Getting into the final is a dream come true for me," said Graves. Ukrainian Mykola Milchev took home the gold medal in the event, followed by Czech Petr Malek with the silver.

Then suddenly, after four years of training and dreaming, it was over. Win or lose, all the athletes could

Thrine Kane shoots in the prone position in the women's 50m rifle three-position qualifying round.

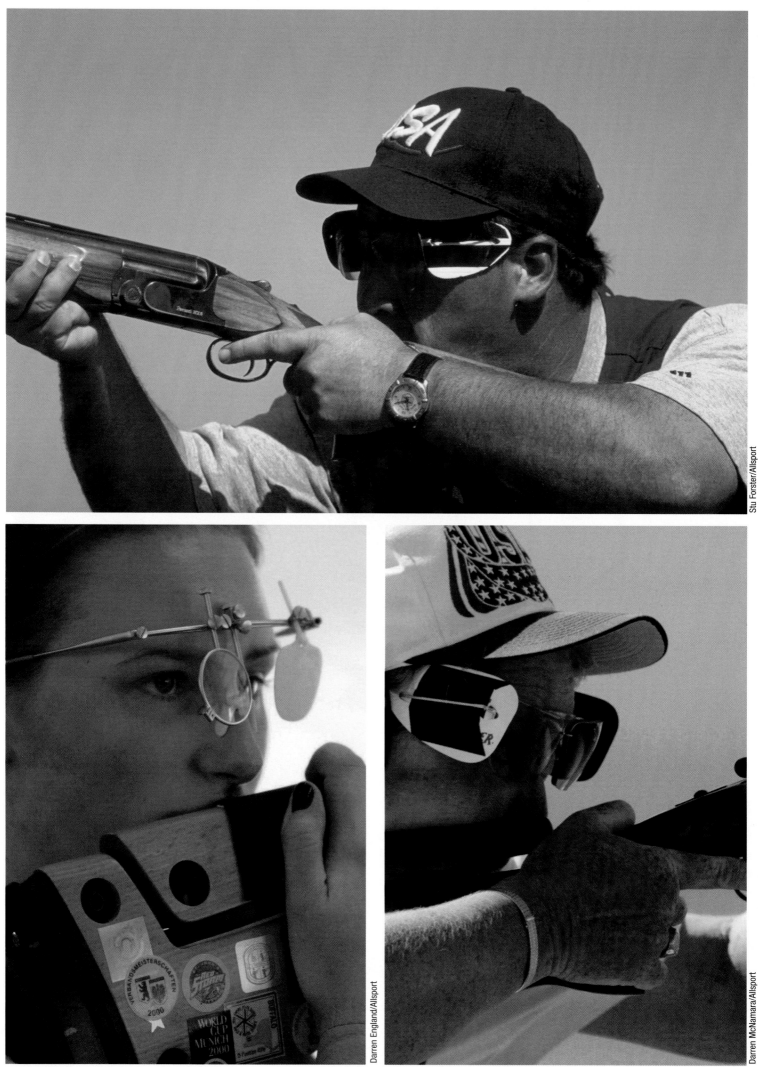

claim the honor few of us will know: to say they are Olympians.

Olympic pistol shooter Bill Demarest summed up the spirit that drives so many athletes. "It wouldn't be fun if it was easy."

Facing page top: Lance Bade aims for the final round in double trap and takes an eventual sixth place.

Facing page botttom left: Thrine Kane prepares to shoot in the standing position in women's 50m rifle three-position.

Facing page botttom right: Cindy Gentry advances to the finals for an eventual sixth place finish in women's trap.

This page, top:Cindy Shenberger aims for a medal but takes fifth place in the skeet shooting final.

Bottom: Shells fly in the men's double trap competition.

Right: Mia Hamm takes the ball to the goal in the semifinal win against Brazil.

Next page: Kuwait's Naser Alothman (right) tries to stop Jeff Agoos and the U.S. team's onslaught, but the U.S. advances with a 3-1 victory over the Kuwaiti team.

SOCCER

By Bryan Chenault (Men) and Aaron Heifetz (Women)

MEN

They came to Australia looking to make a name for themselves. They left having missed a bronze medal by mere inches. But along the way, the men's U.S. Olympic Soccer Team became one of the most surprising and exhilarating stories of the 2000 Olympic Games.

In 11 previous attempts dating back to 1924, the U.S. had never advanced to the second round of Olympic competition. But this time around was different. This team was different.

Thanks to the invention of Major League Soccer in 1996 and the recent and vast development of U.S. Soccer's youth national teams, it was an under-23 team that was the most experienced, yet the youngest team that the U.S. has ever fielded. So, with a team that featured 17 professionals out of 18 players, vastly different from the college all-star teams the U.S. has had in past Games, the U.S. was finally on a level playing field with the rest of the world. Still, the U.S. team was a definite underdog among the 16 teams that qualified.

It only took two games to show the rest of the world that the U.S. was there to play. Against their first two opponents, both early gold medal favorites, the resilient U.S. team survived rough starts to end up dominating their favored competitors, each time drawing even and walking away knowing they were the better team.

In their final preliminary match, a must-win game versus Kuwait, the U.S. built a 2-1 lead before a late goal from teenage scoring sensation Landon Donovan helped the team

Above: Kristine Lilly (left) is pursued by Cidinha of Brazil as Julie Foudy follows in the semifinal match.

Below left: Christie Pearce takes possession in the preliminary game against China.

Below right: Tiffeny Milbrett (right) and Eberechi Opara of Nigeria battle for possession in a preliminary game.

Shaun Botterill/Allsport

Shaun Botterill/Allsport

Tiffeny Milbrett scores the first goal of the tournament for the U.S. in the match against Norway.

Hege Riise of Norway (left), Joy Fawcett (center) and U.S. goalkeeper Siri Mullenix collide defending the goal.

Olympic gold medal opportunity.

As Norway had worked its way back to the final, the scene was set for a clash between the women's soccer superpowers. The U.S. got a dream start as Hamm set up Milbrett for a score just five minutes into the match. But while they pounded at the Norwegian goal for the rest of the half, the U.S. could not get a second score. Norway tied the game just before halftime and then, against the run of play, took the lead with 12 minutes left

in the game. The U.S. battled ferociously for an equalizer, and came up with a heart-stopping goal from Milbrett. Hamm's cross deep in stoppage time found Milbrett's head at the far post and the 5-foot-2 striker sliced her header into the net to tie the game.

Norway did not fold after giving up such a crushing goal and ran with urgency at the U.S. in the sudden death overtime period, scoring a opportunistic goal when Dagney

Mellgren used her upper arm to block Joy Fawcett's attempt to head a ball clear, then tucked her shot underneath goalkeeper Siri Mullinix to end the game, and perhaps an era, in American women's soccer.

The U.S. players earned praise for the way they handled defeat, resigning with grace despite a controversial goal, and conducting themselves with the class and character that has made them among America's favorite athletes.

USA

Dot Richardson gets a hit.

SOFTBALL

U S A

By Bryan McCall

Perseverance and determination became catch phrases for these golden girls as the 2000 Games went down as one of the toughest competitions the team has ever participated in.

Dynamic debuts and a no-hitter from Lori Harrigan vaulted the women to a 6-0 victory over Canada in the first game. Harrigan became the first individual pitcher to record a no-hitter during the Olympic Games, striking out five players and not allowing a walk.

Offensive support was plentiful against Canada as U.S. batters churned out 10 hits, including three

home runs. Crystl Bustos made her Olympic debut, going 3-for-4 including a home run. And Jennifer Brundage, also a first-time Olympian, went 2-for-3, adding her own home run to the tally. The final run of the game came in the sixth inning, when Dr. Dot Richardson delivered a solo homer to right field.

In game two, the U.S. defeated Cuba 3-0. But in game three, squandered opportunities on offense and a defense that finally broke marked the loss to Japan.

In game four, the U.S. defense failed again versus China in a 14-inning affair. Kept at bay through

more than 13 innings by left-handed pitcher Michele Smith, China finally broke through with two outs in the top of the 14th and the U.S. suffered its second loss of the games.

Against Australia, the fifth game went 13 innings and was decided on a two-out home run in the bottom of the frame, giving the host country a 2-1 decision. U.S. pitcher Lisa Fernandez continued the team's run of exceptional but unlucky performances from inside the circle. The right-hander set an Olympic record with 25 strikeouts, breaking the mark of 19 set by teammate Michele Smith the previous evening

Above: Team USA gives thanks for their win in the final against Japan.

Left: Jennifer Brundage (right) slides into Misako Ando of Japan.

Lower left: Dr. Dot Richardson and a Chinese player scramble for the base.

Below: Stacey Nuveman (left) and Lisa Fernandez celebrate the win over Australia.

Above: Vilma Alvarez of Cuba reaches first base before she is tagged by Sheila Douty.

Previous page:
Top: Christa Williams pitches against Japan in their early meeting.
Lower left: Lori Harrigan pitches against Canada in the preliminary round.
Lower right: Lisa Fernandez throws for the gold against Japan in the Grand Final.

and allowed just two hits and one walk.

In game six, the U.S. team maintained its flair for strong pitching, with Lori Harrigan and Christa Williams combining for a one-hitter. The U.S. offense reappeared as they defeated New Zealand and moved one step closer to the medal rounds.

An unprecedented three-game skid midway through the round-robin portion of the tournament schedule forced the United States into a true elimination game, where the winner advanced and the loser was retired from the competition. Facing the possibility of not being able to defend its gold medal, the U.S. team defeated Italy 6-0 to secure the fourth and final slot in the medal round.

In the opening semi-final game, Stacey Nuveman hit a three-run home run in the bottom of the 10th inning to lift the U.S. to a 3-0 win over China and keep its hopes alive for a second gold medal. In the bronze medal game, knowing a win would advance the team to the gold medal round while a loss would send them home with bronze, Lisa Fernandez and Dot Richardson rose to the occasion. Fernandez pitched a one-hit shutout with 13 strikeouts and Richardson delivered an RBI-single to edge Australia 1-0 and secure a spot in the gold medal game. The win completed a three-game sweep of the teams that had defeated the U.S. during the round-robin competition. The women went on to defend their gold medal, beating Japan 2-1 in eight innings.

Japan initiated the scoring when Reika Utsugi drilled a line drive home run in the fourth inning, but the United States responded in the bottom of the fifth. In that frame, Michele Smith was hit by a pitch, moved to second on a ground out from Sheila Douty and scored on a single from Nuveman.

The game-winning run was not pretty but it was effective; it came on a dropped fly ball hit by Laura Berg.

Above: Christie Ambrosi throws the ball in from the outfield in the preliminary match-up with Japan.

Lower left: A jubilant Dot Richardson heads to the dugout.

Lower center: Crystl Bustos throws home against Japan in the final.

Lower right: Stacey Nuveman celebrates a U.S. run in a tough match with China.

Above: Jennifer Brundage is on base and will make it home against Japan in the preliminary round.

Above right: Lisa Fernandez winds up against Australia in the preliminary round.

Shiori Koseki fell backward and dropped Berg's shot to deep left field, allowing Jennifer McFalls to score from second.

The loss was the first of the Games for Japan, going 7-0 in round-robin competition and then defeating Australia in the opening game of the medal round to advance straight to the gold medal game. Its second-place finish garners Japan its first Olympic medal in softball.

133

Previous page, top: Misty Hyman celebrates with her teammate Kaitlin Sandeno after winning gold in the women's 200-meter butterfly.

Previous page, bottom: Training partners Anthony Ervin (left) and Gary Hall Jr. tie for gold in the men's 50-meter freestyle final.

Top: As "The Star Spangled Banner" plays and Old Glory is raised at the 200-meter butterfly medal ceremony, gold medal winner Misty Hyman's face is super-imposed over the flag on a giant TV screen.

Middle: Amy Van Dyken, Dara Torres and Courtney Shealy cheer for Jenny Thompson (not pictured) to shatter the world record and take the gold medal in the women's 4x100-meter freestyle relay.

Left: Kristy Kowal swims to a silver medal finish in the women's 200-meter breaststroke.

Next page: Lenny Krayzelburg starts the men's 200-meter backstroke semifinal.

Hamish Blair/Allsport

Top: Brooke Bennett increases her lead down the long course to the gold medal in the women's 800-meter freestyle final.

Center: A very happy Agnes Kovacs of Hungary (left) celebrates her gold medal performance with bronze medalist Amanda Beard after the women's 200-meter breaststroke final.

Bottom left: Kyle Salyards looks on during a training session before the start of the Games.

Bottom right: Chad Carvin signals to the crowd after winning his heat in the men's 400-meter freestyle.

Next page: Tom Wilkens qualifies for the men's 200-meter individual medley final where he eventually takes the bronze medal.

Matt Turner/Allsport

Al Bello/Allsport

Al Bello/Allsport

Al Bello/Allsport

Al Bello/Allsport

Youngster Megan Quann, just 16, won the 100-meter breaststroke and also helped the team of BJ Bedford, Torres and Thompson take gold in world record time in the 400-meter medley relay.

Tom Dolan defended his title in the 400-meter individual medley in decisive fashion, smashing his own world record from 1994 in the process. He also claimed silver in the 200-meter individual medley.

Tom Malchow, who won silver in the 200-meter butterfly as the youngest team member in Atlanta, came back to win the gold in Sydney. This year's youngest member, 15-year-old Michael Phelps, showed great promise in the same event finishing fifth in this Olympic Games.

The U.S. team had a couple of 1-2 showings with Erik Vendt taking silver to Dolan's gold in the 400-meter individual medley, Diana Munz securing silver to Bennett's gold in the 800-meter freestyle and Aaron Peirsol earning silver in the 200-meter backstroke.

Kristy Kowal and Ed Moses both won silver in the 200-meter breaststroke and 100-meter breaststroke, respectively. Ervin, Neil Walker, Jason Lezak and Hall earned silver in the 400-meter freestyle relay, while Scott Goldblatt, Josh Davis, Jamie Rauch and Klete Keller took silver in the 800-meter freestyle relay. Amanda Beard was the bronze medalist in the 200-meter breaststroke.

Also earning bronze was Keller in the 400-meter freestyle, Kaitlin Sandeno in the 800-meter freestyle,

Previous pages: Jenny Thompson and Dara Torres go head to head in the women's 100-meter butterfly. They finished with Torres in third place for the bronze medal and Thompson in fifth place.

Top: Tom Wilkens qualifies for the men's 200-meter individual medley final where he eventually took the bronze medal.

Middle: Misty Hyman on her way to the gold medal in the women's 200m butterfly.

Bottom: Tom Dolan comes up for air on his way to the silver medal in men's 200-meter individual medley.

world. Poe was ranked number one in the world when she entered the 2000 United States Olympic Taekwondo Team Trials. She dislocated her left knee before her final match where she would face her best friend of eleven years, Esther Kim. Kim bowed out of the competition so that Poe would make the Olympic team without having to fight her with an injured leg.

Poe did not finish her day at the Olympic Games as she had hoped, but she had a seat with her friend Kim, International Olympic Committee President Juan Antonio Samaranch, Henry Kissinger, and IOC Vice President Un Yong Kim to watch Lauren Burns of Australia and Michail Mouroutsos of Greece win the first Olympic gold medals for Taekwondo.

Juan Miguel Moreno of Miami, FL, saw his dreams of another Olympic medal die when Joseph Salim of Hungary defeated him in his first round match. Barbara Kunkel suffered the same fate after a first round bye when Mirjam Mueskens of the Netherlands defeated her in the welterweight division.

The United States was one of only six countries to qualify a full team for the 2000 Olympic Games. The success of the sport gives the world something to look forward to at the 2004 Olympic Games in Athens, Greece.

Top: Steven Lopez kicks Joon-Sik Sin of Korea to become the first American to win gold in Taekwondo.

Middle: Barbara Kunkel attacks but eventually falls to Mirjam Mueskens of the Netherlands in the preliminary round.

Bottom: Carlo Massimino of Australia puts up a good fight but is defeated by Steven Lopez.

Above: The queen of the court, Venus Williams, gives an Olympic-sized effort on her way to the gold medal.

Below: The Sydney Games left their mark on everything down to the tennis balls.

TENNIS

By Randy Walker

Sports fans grew familiar with the sight of Venus Williams winning tennis tournaments in the summer of 2000. She leaped in the air with glee on the lawns of Wimbledon after winning her first Grand Slam singles title in July. She waved to the boisterous spectators in New York after winning the U.S. Open in September.

But it was Olympic gold that brought tears to the eyes of the 20-year-old superstar.

The 6-2, 6-4 defeat of Russia's up-and-coming star Elena Dementieva in the gold medal women's singles match not only solidified Williams' domination of women's tennis in 2000, but also fulfilled a dream that she never thought would come true.

"You have so many opportunities to win the Wimbledons and the Grand Slams, but this gold medal is just every four years," said Williams. "This is the one moment in time for my country, for the team, for my family and for me."

Williams appeared in disbelief as she stepped on the medal podium and received what she later would jokingly call her "favorite Olympic pin." International Olympic Committee Vice President Anita DeFranz placed the Olympic gold medal around Williams' neck, which resulted in a beaming smile that shined as brightly as her medal. Williams wiped away the tears as "The Star Spangled Banner" played and the U.S. flag was rose above her head.

A day after her singles triumph, Williams was able to share another "moment in time" with younger sister Serena Williams as the duo won gold in women's doubles. "To have a victory like this with Serena, my sister, my best friend, has been really, really good," Venus said. The Williams sisters became the first set of sisters ever to share Olympic tennis gold. The "Olympic double"

Seles packs a bronze-medal-winning wallop during the women's singles tournament.

for Venus put her in the company of 1924 Olympian Helen Wills as the only woman to win Olympic gold medals in singles and doubles.

The gold medal sweep by the U.S. women marked the third consecutive Olympiad in which American women have capitalized on all gold medal opportunities.

Also making the most of her Olympic opportunity was Monica Seles. She finally won her first Olympic medal after 11 years for competitive international play and nine Grand Slam singles titles. Seles cruised into the semifinals winning three of her four matches in less than an hour before losing to teammate Venus Williams in a hard-fought, three-set thriller. Seles then out-slugged Australian teenager Jelena Dokic for the bronze medal.

With every story of Olympic glory also come stories of unfulfilled dreams and disappointment. Defending Olympic gold medallist Lindsay Davenport entered the Games hoping to become the first player to defend an Olympic gold medal in singles. However, after a few days of practice, Davenport began feeling extreme soreness in her left foot. After the first round of competition, Davenport was forced to withdraw from the event.

"Not be able to perform in a tournament that will probably be the highlight of my career is just devastating," said a somber Davenport. "I've had to pull out of a lot of tournaments before, but obviously nothing compares quite to this one."

The U.S. men's team featured six veteran players whose average age was a very mature 29. Todd Martin, the brightest medal hope for the United States, entered his first Olympic Games fresh from the semifinals of the U.S. Open the week before the Olympic Opening Ceremonies. However, the 30-year-old had difficulty re-charging his body and was defeated in the opening round of the Games by

Germany's Rainer Schuttler.

Michael Chang, the only former Olympian on the U.S. men's team, also struggled in his first round match, falling to Sebastien Lareau of Canada. Vince Spadea, a late substitution for Andre Agassi who withdrew due to family matters, was another first round Olympic casualty, falling to Australia's Olympic torch-bearing hero, Patrick Rafter.

Top: Vince Spadea keeps his eye on the ball but eventually falls to tough competition in the first round of the men's singles tournament.

Above: The Williams sisters, Venus (left) and Serena, form an unbeatable team in doubles competition becoming the first pair of sisters to share Olympic doubles gold.

Right: Lindsay Davenport is determined to defend her gold medal but falls victim to injury after the first round.

Clive Brunskill/Allsport

In doubles, medal contenders Alex O'Brien and Jared Palmer also lost their opening round match to Mark Knowles and Mark Merklein of the Bahamas.

Thirty-one-year old Jeff Tarango was the oldest man to play Olympic tennis for the United States since Titanic survivor Richard Norris Williams in 1924. He was the lone U.S. competitor to advance to the second round when he defeated Bolivia's Hector Camacho. Tarango's - and the U.S. men's - hopes of an Olympic medal faded as Argentina's Mariano Zabaleta eliminated the mercucial Tarango in straight sets in the second round.

USA
⊕⊕⊕

Left: Venus is the picture of serenity as she prepares to unleash an explosive serve.

Below: The New South Wales Tennis Center at Sydney Olympic Park is the setting for American triumphs as well as disappointments.

Nick Wilson/Allsport

Joanna Zeiger gets a hand from the crowd on her way to fourth place in Women's Triathlon.

TRIATHLON

By B.J. Hoeptner

WOMEN

The inaugural Olympic triathlon competition at the 2000 Olympic Games in Sydney drew huge crowds as fans were lined up to 15 deep along the course. U.S. triathletes Joanna Zeiger of Baltimore, MD, Sheila Taormina, of Livonia, MI, and Jennifer Gutierrez of San Antonio, TX, did not bring home any medals, but they can be proud of their fourth, sixth and 13th place finishes.

"We had three girls in the first pack," said U.S. triathlete Joanna Zeiger, "and two finishers in the

top 10. I think we put on an unbelievable performance."

The weather was sunny but cool as the triathletes dove into Sydney Harbor for the first leg of the race. As expected, Olympic swimming gold medalist Taormina jumped out to a 50-meter lead. After a quick transition from swim to bike, Taormina extended her lead, but realized she could not hold it without her teammates' help.

"I said to myself, 'All right, enjoy the crowd. Let the pack catch you because you know they're going to,'" Taormina said.

Gutierrez took a brief lead on the bike, but lost count of the laps and took almost 30 seconds to transition from bike to run.

"I was not really paying attention," Gutierrez said. "All of a sudden, I realized the other athletes were taking off their shoes."

Gutierrez and Taormina helped Zeiger get near the front of the pack on the bike, but on the first lap of the run, Zeiger had to adjust her pace when she dropped her asthma inhaler. Without it, she knew she had to be cautious saying, "I could feel my

heart rate going up.
I had to back off a little bit so I would not have an asthma attack."

Brigitte McMahon of Switzerland won the gold medal in 2:00:40.52. Australia's Michellie Jones took silver in 2:00:42.55 and Switzerland's Magali Messmer won bronze in 2:01:08.

MEN

The men's triathlon team had troubles as well. Hunter Kemper of Longwood, FL, led the U.S. team, but finished in 17th-place. Ryan Bolton of Gillette, WY, finished 25th and teammate Nick Radkewich of Detroit, MI, placed 40th.

"When I got seventh at World's earlier this year," said Kemper, "I felt like I just kept getting faster and faster until I was flying at the end. Today it was like, man, the legs just were not there."

Bolton was involved in a crash on the sixth lap of the bike. "It was not that bad really," said Bolton, who had a scrape on his leg and a hole in his uniform. Bolton said the crash happened too fast for him to avoid it. "It was on an incline and riders are so close, it kind of causes a chain reaction."

"The crowd out there was an amazing experience," Radkewich said. "All the Aussie fans really cheered for everybody. The made up the majority of the crowd, but the Aussies cheered for every single person."

Simon Whitfield of Canada took home the gold in 1:48:24. Stephan Vuckovic of Germany won silver in 1:48:37.58 and Jan Rehula of the Czech Republic took bronze in 1:48:46.64.

Top: With one of the world's most famous landmarks as their backdrop, competitors in Men's Triathlon tear through the waters of Sydney Harbor.

Middle: A sea of the world's finest female triathletes awaits the signal to plunge into Sydney Harbor at the start of the first Olympic Triathlon competition.

Left: The crowd in front of the Sydney Opera House cheers as triathletes complete the transistion from swim to bike.

Dain Blanton (left) watches his teammate Eric Fonoimoana spike past Ricardo Santos of Brazil in the men's beach volleyball final where the duo took the gold medal.

VOLLEYBALL

By Gavin Markovits

BEACH VOLLEYBALL

By all accounts, it was the most spectacular venue of the 2000 Games. Sun, sand, surf, and exciting play by 48 of the best beach volleyball athletes in the world highlighted the Olympic beach volleyball tournament on Bondi Beach.

Men

The men's competition was led by the two best teams in the world, Brazil's duo of Emanuel Rego and Jose Loiola and the duo of Ricardo Santos and Ze'Marco de Melo. And the U.S. pairs, Dain Blanton and Eric Fonoimoana and Rob Heidger and Kevin Wong were aiming for them.

In the first round, the No. 1 seeded team of Julien Prosser and Lee Zahner of Australia were upset 15-12 by Juan Ibarra and Joel Sotelo of Mexico, sending them down into the contender's bracket.

The U.S. pairing of Heidger and Wong had lost their first round match as well to join Prosser and Zahner in the contender's bracket. Prosser and Zahner fought their way back into the main draw with wins of 15-12 over Jan Kvalheim and Bjorn Maaseide of Norway, and 15-11 over Heidger and Wong.

Heidger and Wong, however, were the "lucky losers" of the contender's bracket. As the team with the best point ratio of the losers, the U.S. duo also got to go

back to the main draw.

In the next round, Heidger and Wong gave new meaning to the term "lucky loser," as their opponents, Ibarra and Sotelo of Mexico had to forfeit due to an injury.

In the next round, the two U.S teams faced off against one another with Blanton and Fonoimoana coming out on top 15-3. That duo then advanced to the finals with a 15-12 win over Joao Brenha and Miguel Maia of Portugal.

Heading into the final, the odds favored the Brazilian team of Santos and Ze'Marco. But Blanton and Fonoimoana were focused. They were going to fight as hard as they could. And they did. When the dust

Darren McNamara/Allsport

Gary M. Prior/Allsport

Holly McPeak catches some air as she returns against Brazil in the quarterfinal match.

Dain Blanton (right) and Eric Fonoimoana celebrate their semifinal victory over Portugal and their shot at the gold medal.

settled in the final, they had won the gold medal in a thrilling, 12-11, 12-9 victory. Santos and Ze'Marco took silver.

In the bronze medal match, Jorg Ahmann and Axel Hager of Germany defeated Brenha and Maia 12-9, 12-6 to claim the medal.

The biggest winner was the sport of beach volleyball, which was showcased in a spectacular venue on a gorgeous beach by the best athletes in the sport for all the world to see.

A great tournament, a great Olympics. It doesn't get much better than that.

Women

The U.S. women's teams, two of the top teams in the world, were playing great and were a strong possibility to medal going into the Games.

The USA's No. 1 team of Annett Davis and Jenny Johnson Jordan had a strong summer season, winning FIVB events in Marseilles, France, taking second in Italy and third in Mexico, as well as winning tournaments at home. They were playing strong and seemed ready for the Games.

The USA's No. 2 team was virtually unknown beginning the season. But heading into the Games, Misty May and Holly McPeak were

arguably the hottest pair in the world and the team to beat.

Once the Games started, however, both pairs seemed out of sync, but they were still winning their matches.

In their first match, the duo of Davis and Johnson Jordan struggled to a 15-13 win over Australians Sarah Straton and Annette Huygens Tholen. They played a little better in the next round, besting Dalixia Fernandez Grossat and Tamara Larrea Peraza of Cuba 15-9.

May and McPeak played a strong first match, defeating Martina Hudcova and Tereza Tobiasova of the Czech Republic, 15-5. Despite a strong lead in their next match, they had trouble closing out the Italian team of Daniela Gattelli/Lucilla Perrotta, but eventually pulled out a 15-13 victory.

Both teams' struggles continued into their next matches, which turned out to be their last.

Davis and Johnson Jordan ran into Teru Saiki and Yukiko Takahashi of Japan. In a 48-minute match, Saiki and Takahashi defeated Davis and Johnson Jordan 15-9 to end the pair's quest for a medal.

May and McPeak also faced a tough team, Brazil's Sandra Pires and Adriana Samuel, former gold and silver medalists. The May/McPeak duo played well throughout the match, taking leads of 2-0 and 8-6, but fell to Pires and Samuel 16-14 in 49 minutes.

Both U.S. women's teams finished fifth, but they still enjoyed their Olympic experience. "The

Top: Holly McPeak (left) and Misty May celebrate their defeat of Czech duo Martina Hudcova and Tereza Tobiasova.

Bottom left: Jennifer Jordan Johnson makes contact during the 1/8 final against Cuba.

Bottom right: Robert Heidger Jr. spikes against Canada in the elimination round.

Eric Fonoimoana waits for a serve in the quarterfinal match.

medal is what we played for," Johnson Jordan said, "But it's not the most important thing."

Australians Natalie Cook and Kerri Pottharst claimed the gold medal while Brazil's Adriana Behar and Shelda Bede took silver and Sandra Pires and Adriana Samuel took bronze.

It was a tough tournament for the U.S. women, but the future is definitely looking bright. Both teams are still young and improving and other strong U.S. players are emerging. By the 2004 Games in Athens, Greece, they will be even better and the U.S. women will once again go for the gold.

INDOOR VOLLEYBALL

Women
The U.S. Women's Olympic Volleyball Team narrowly missed a medal. Yet, despite the disappointment, the team had many reasons to be proud. Entering the Games as the 10th-ranked team in the world, the Red, White and Blue upset No. 4 China and No. 8 Croatia in pool play to advance to the quarterfinals.

Team USA opened the tournament looking nervous, but settled quickly to outlast the tough Chinese. Danielle Scott pounded 17 kills and added six blocks while Logan Tom posted 12 kills and five blocks.

In their next match, Team USA dominated from the start, putting Kenya away in just 62 minutes. Demetria Sance led the team with 16 kills on 25 attacks.

The U.S. then easily rolled over No. 8 Croatia. The key was the U.S. team's ability to stop Croatia's Barbara Jelic, posting eight blocks on the tournament's best scorer.

After cruising past the host Australians, Team USA met Brazil, the defending bronze medalists, to battle for first place in Pool A. With a four-set victory, the Brazilians sent the U.S into the quarterfinals where they would face Korea.

Danielle Scott (No. 2) puts a kill on Brazil in the preliminary round.

Jed Jacobsohn/Allsport

Michael Lambert returns against Russia during the indoor volleyball preliminaries.

At right: John Hyden (left) and Thomas Hoff attempt a block against Yugoslavia.

In an epic five-set match, Team USA outlasted No. 5 Korea. Scott posted 26 kills and five blocks, while Tom added 22 kills. Stacy Sykora recorded a career-high of 26 digs.

A five-set loss to No. 2 Russia dropped the Americans into the bronze medal match where No. 3 Brazil dispatched the U.S. in three sets. Cuba claimed its third consecutive gold medal with a come-from-behind victory over Russia.

Scott led Team USA and the tournament with 34 blocks. She added 98 kills. Nineteen-year-old Tom was spectacular in her first Olympic Games with 96 kills, 64 digs and 17 blocks. Libero Stacy Sykora ranked second in the Games with 113 digs.

WATER POLO

USA

By Eric Velazquez

WOMEN

Years spent and sacrifices made. But when the crowds had quieted, the lights had dimmed and the waters had settled, it was silver, not gold, that draped around the necks of the 13 members of the U.S. women's water polo team. It was a remarkable achievement, but not the ending that Coach Baker and company had scripted over the last few months.

When the final horn sounded in that night's gold medal game, there was no changing the unsettling fact, no denying the scoreboard. Australia had come out on the top end of a game that will go down in the annals of water polo history. The first gold medals ever handed out in women's water polo went to the host country, their red, white, and blue clad guests

watching from only feet away.

And it all came down to the final seconds.

Yvette Higgins fired the shot heard 'round the world that night, burying a shot from seven meters out to shatter a 3-3 impasse with 0.2 seconds left in the game. The goal sent the record crowd of 17,000-plus into an uproar, with chants of "Aussie, Aussie, Aussie-Oy, Oy, Oy" and "Waltzing Matilda" barely audible over the madness.

In a game that will be remembered for generations to come, the score was knotted three times, including once in the final minute of the game.

It looked as if the game was destined for overtime, but with 1.3 seconds left, U.S. captain Julie Swail

Top: Tony Azevedo fires a shot against Russia in a close quarterfinal match that ended with Russia on top, 11-10.

Above: Maureen O'Toole controls the ball in the preliminary round meeting with Australia, her eventual opponent in the gold medal game.

Next page, top: Chris Oeding signals his teammates in the preliminary game versus Yugoslavia.

Next page, middle left: Kathy Sheedy and her Australian opponent battle for possession in a hard fought gold medal game.

Next page, middle right: Julie Swail works the ball against Canada in the preliminary round resulting in an 8-8 tie.

Next page, bottom: Kyle Kopp (left) keeps the ball away from his Yugoslavian opponent.

was called for an ejection, stopping the clock. The ensuing free pass ended up in the hands of 22-year-old Yvette Higgins who caught and shot from the point about seven meters out. The ball, which was fired high left, was tipped by Coralie Simmons and goalkeeper Bernice Orwig before finding its home in the cage with 0.2 seconds left.

Australia had won the gold.

The enormous crowd support and media turnout sent a jolt through the wide world of women's water polo, a sport that has waited 100 years to join its male counterpart on the Olympic roster of games.

And the U.S. women's water polo team had succeeded beyond anyone's wildest expectations. They were a part of history.

But silver is hardly something to look down on. They are an amazingly talented group of women who waited their turn to secure their spot in the books, women whose aquatic skill is only outdone by their bright eyes, luminous smiles, upright character, unrelenting fortitude and unbelievable persistence. Their cloud definitely has a silver lining.

And a good portion of them will be back for Athens in 2004.

MEN

Back in June of 2000, U.S. men's water polo head coach John Vargas called this year's team "the most physically talented team" in recent U.S. water polo history. They had the bodies, the talent and the experience to bring home some hardware; it would just be a matter of putting

Top: Ericka Lorenz pushes to the ball during the preliminary match against Russia. The USA defeated Russia 6-4.

Middle: Chris Oeding in action against the Netherlands.

Bottom: Brenda Villa looks to pass during the match against Canada in the preliminary round.

Hamish Blair/Allsport

Daren McNamara/Allsport

Scott Barbour/Allsport

them all together for nine days in Sydney.

Unfortunately, the Olympic gods had other plans in mind.

The U.S., despite strong showings against some of the world's best teams, finished sixth in the tournament, one better than its seventh place finish in Atlanta, but one place lower than needed for an automatic qualification at next year's World Championships.

The U.S. will be back in 2004 in hopes of a return to the medal stand. The U.S. brought home two medals in the 1980s, and has six total. And with a solid base of returners led by young Tony Azevedo and a healthy reservoir of recruits to choose from, Team USA could be bringing home number seven.

USA

Left: Julie Swail controls the ball in the match between Australia and the USA.

Below: U.S. Coach Guy William Baker addresses his team during a break in the gold medal match against Australia.

Clive Brunskill/Allsport

Above: Tara Nott, who only took up the sport after the 1996 Games, becomes the first gold medalist in women's weightlifting.
Next page: Seventeen-year-old Cheryl Haworth lifts for the bronze medal in the women's 75+ kg division.

By Christine M. Hyde

The 2000 Games were historic for the sport of weightlifting thanks to the inclusion of women for the first time. But for the United States women, these Games were golden.

Tara Nott and Robin Goad competed for the U.S. in the 48 kg (105 lbs) class. Emotions were high especially for Goad, a pioneer in the sport and the only World Champion on the 2000 team. After 17 years of competition, her Olympic dreams were finally coming true.

Goad was quickly overshadowed by her teammate, Tara Nott, who hoisted a total of 185.0 kg (407 lbs) over her head, snatching 82.5 kg

(181.5 lbs) and clean & jerking 102.5 kg (225.5 lbs), to tie Indonesia's Raema Lisa Rumbewas for the silver medal. However, since Nott weighed-in at one pound less than her competitor, she was awarded the silver, and Rumbewas took the bronze. Goad finished sixth with a total of 177.5 kg (390.5 lbs).

A few days later, the silver lining to Nott's Olympic experience turned golden. Bulgarian gold medalist Izabela Dragneva was disqualified after a positive doping test and Nott would go down in history as the first gold medalist in women's Olympic weightlifting.

Nott missed her new medal ceremony to watch 17-year-old teammate Cheryl Haworth's competition. "It was really honored when I found out what she had given up to see me lift," said Haworth. To recognize her dedication, the U.S. Olympic Committee held a special ceremony to present her with her gold medal.

Haworth seized the bronze medal in the 75+ kg (165+ lbs) weight class after breaking three American records. The young lifter, who took time off from high school to compete, snatched 125.0 kg (275 lbs) and clean & jerked 145.0 kg (319 lbs), for a

Scott Barbour/Allsport

Scott Barbour/Allsport

Scott Barbour/Allsport

record-breaking total of 279.0 kg (594 lbs). Afterwords, Haworth watched China's Meiyuan Ding and Poland's Agata Wrobel break eight world records as they battled for the gold medal.

Cara Heads-Lane competed in the 75 kg (165 lbs) weight class, finishing by lifting a total of 222.5 kg (489.5 lbs).

The U.S. Men's Olympic Weightlifting Team was a contingent of only two athletes. Oscar Chaplin III, the reigning Junior World Champion in the 77 kg (170 lbs) weight class entered as the top-ranked U.S. male lifter, while super-heavyweight Shane Hamman came in at number two.

Chaplin made three of his six attempts, for a total of 335.0 kg (737 lbs), finishing in 12th place. Hamman broke three American records en route to a 420.0 kg (924 lbs) total and a 10th-place finish.

USA
♢♢♢

Previous page: Shane Hamman controls, releases and celebrates a successful lift making him the top U.S. finisher in his weight class.

Top: Robin Goad, the veteran of the U.S. women's weightlifting team, shows excellent form in the Snatch event.

Above: Oscar Chaplin III lifts to become the highest U.S. finisher in the 77 kg weight class.

WRESTLING

By Gary Abbott

Rulon Gardner surprises everyone by taking the gold from the world's greatest Greco-Roman wrestler, Alexandre Karelin of Russia, who was undefeated throughout his 13-year career.

If one thing was determined at the 2000 Olympic wrestling competition, it is that the United States remains a superpower in the sport.

The U.S. haul at the Sydney Games was seven medals in 16 weight classes, including one gold, three silver and three bronze. But, what immediately became the story of the Sydney Olympic Games was the performance of Greco-Roman super heavyweight Rulon Gardner. In the gold medal finals with the entire world watching, the son of a Wyoming dairy farmer defeated the world's greatest wrestler, three-time Olympic Champion Alexandre Karelin of Russia, unbeaten in 13 years of competition.

This victory was monumental, not only within the sport of wrestling but in the entire sports community since Karelin was looking to end his unprecedented career with a fourth gold medal. IOC President Juan Antonio Samaranch was on hand to present the medal and the world media was in attendance, all expecting salute Karelin. But Gardner changed the plan and rewrote history.

Gardner won 1-0 in overtime, scoring the only point in the match when Karelin released his lock from the clinch position first. Gardner wore down the Russian star with his constant pressure attack and his ability to stop Karelin's patented and

powerful reverse body lift.

Joining Gardner in the Greco-Roman medal tally were silver medalist Matt Linland and bronze medalist Garrett Lowney.

Lindland made an amazing run for the gold, before losing a tight 3-0 decision to Mourat Kardanov of Russia in the gold-medal finals.

Lowney, the youngest member of the U.S. wrestling team at 20 years old, made a breakthrough performance in his first major international event on the senior level. His victory over five-time World Champion Gogui Koguouachvili of Russia will be remembered for many years on the international wrestling circuit.

Billy Strickland/Allsport

Billy Strickland/Allsport

Lowney jumped to an early lead, but Koguachvili tied the bout at 3-3. In overtime, Lowney worked behind Koguachivili and lauched him for a five-point back supplay throw and an 8-3 victory. Five points is the highest possible score of any wrestling move, and Lowney hit it against the top athlete in his weight.

Lowney moved through the quarterfinals and, despite a shoulder and neck injury, posted a solid 3-0 overtime win in the bronze medal match over Konstantinos Thanos of Greece, making an outstanding first impression on the international sports scene.

Also scoring clutch performances for the U.S. team were sixth place finishers Jim Gruenwald at 57 kg and Kevin Bracken at 63 kg.

The freestyle team contributed four medals to the effort, with one gold, one silver and two bronze medals.

Sammie Henson, a 1998 World Champion, competed with power and intensity throughout the Games, winning his first four bouts before dropping a tight 4-3 decision to Namik Abdulayev of Azerbaijan in the gold-medal finals. The silver medal won by Henson was the 100th U.S. freestyle Olympic medal in the modern Olympic Games, a tremendous milestone for the sport.

Brandon Slay had a tremendous performance which rocked the freestyle wrestling world in his first World-level competition for the U.S., with four straight wins before losing the gold-medal match to 1994 World Champion Alexander Leipold of Germany, 4-0. On October 23, 2000, the International Olympic Committee stripped Leipold of his medal for testing positive for steroids, and Slay received the gold.

After opening with a 4-1 decision

Above left: Gardner and Karelin battle for the gold in Greco-Roman wrestling.

Right: Gardner emerges the victor and declares his win to the crowd at the Sydney Convention Centre.

over Bulgaria's Plamen Paskalev, Slay drew 1996 Olympic champion and three-time World Champion Bouvaissa Saitiev of Russia, considered by many to be the top freestyler in the world. Slay quickly jumped to a 3-0 lead on Saitiev, but the Russian responded to tie the score at 3-3 in regulation. In sudden death overtime, Slay scored the winning takedown for an upset victory.

Brands, a two-time World Champion competing in his first Olympic Games, made a comeback from retirement to chase his Olympic dream. He won his pool competition with a pin over Abil Ibragimov of Kazakhstan and an 8-1 win over Chvista Polychoronidis of Greece. In the quarterfinal, Brands won a close 3-2 bout against David Pogosian of Georgia.

In the semifinal, he was edged 6-5 by 1998 World Champion Ali Reza Dabier of Iran in a spectacular match. Dabier jumped to an early lead and Brands made a valiant comeback effort, falling short by one point. In the bronze-medal match, he stopped Damir Zakhartdinov of Uzbekistan, 3-2.

McIlravy, a two-time World medalist, won his pool competition with an injury default win over Ibo Oziti of Nigeria, and a 6-3 win over veteran Yuksel Sanli of Turkey.

Top: Terry Brands (red) and Abil Ibragimov of Kazakhstan (blue) in close quarters during the Men's 58kg freestyle wrestling.

Middle: Garrett Lowney (red) is lifted by Konstantinos Thanos of Greece during Men's 97kg Greco-Roman Wrestling.

Right: Kevin Bracken grapples with Varteres Samourgachev of Russia in Men's 63kg class quarterfinals.

Next page: A birds-eye view of the action during the Greco-Roman Wrestling Pool Elimination.

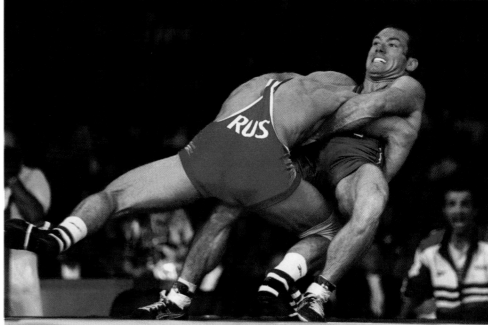

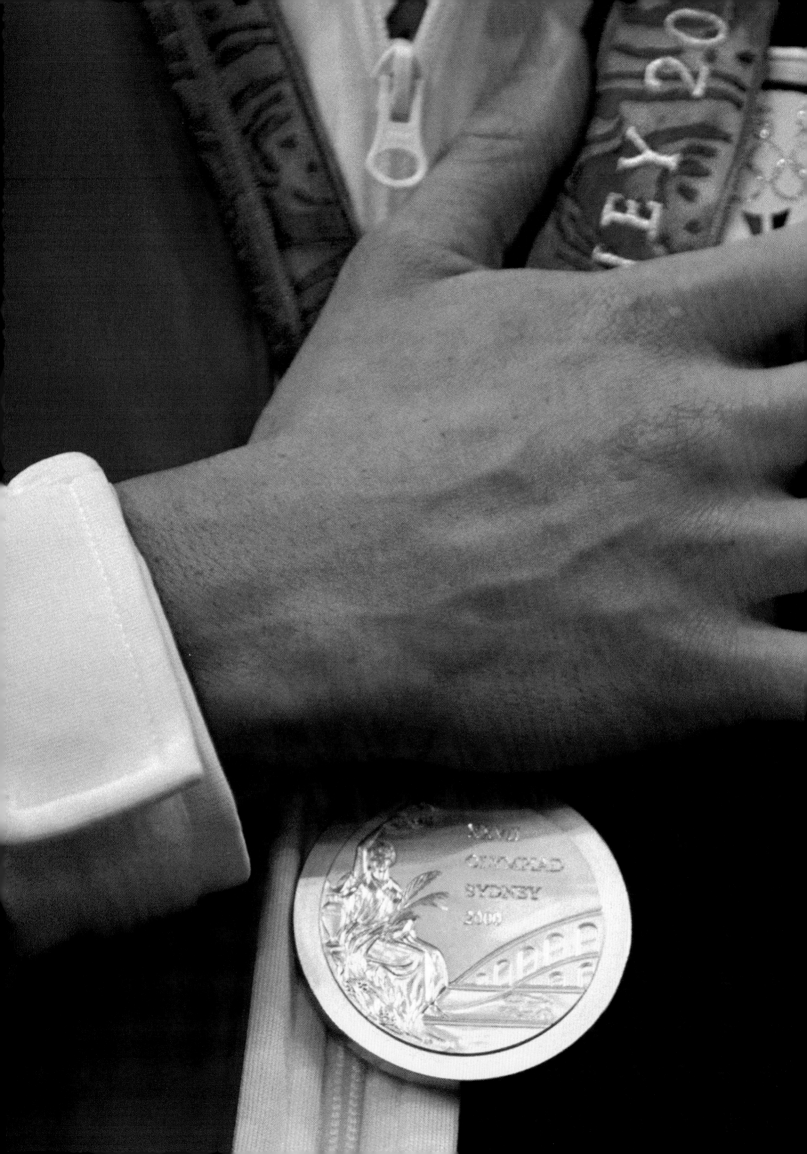

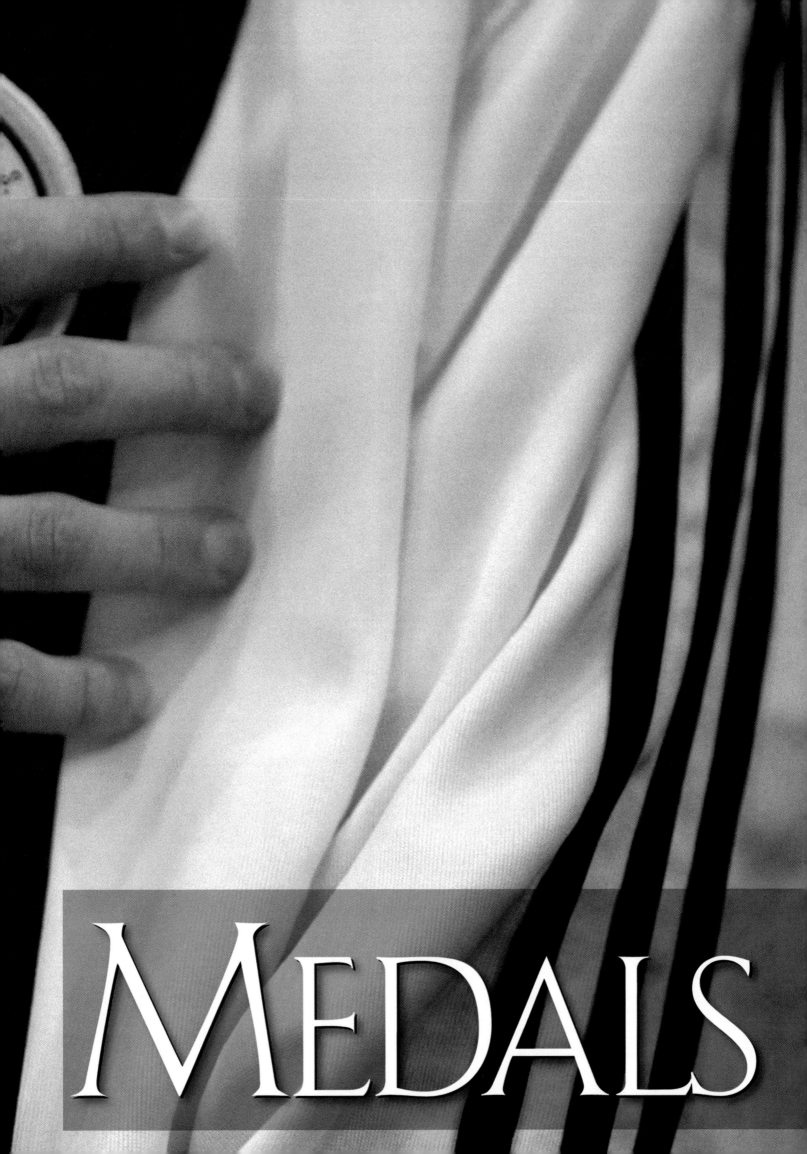

MEDALS

9/16/00 Shooting, Women's 10m Air Rifle: Nancy Johnson, Gold

9/16/00 Swimming, Men's 400m Freestyle: Klete Keller (right), Bronze

9/16/00 Swimming, Men's 4x100m Freestyle Relay:
Gary Hall, Jr., Anthony Ervin, Jason Lezak and Neil Walker, Silver

9/17/00 Swimming, Men's 100m Breaststroke: Ed Moses (left), Silver

9/16/00 Swimming, Women's 4x100m Freestyle Relay: Amy Van Dyken, Dara
Torres, Courtney Shealy and Jenny Thompson, Gold

9/17/00 Swimming, Women's 400m Freestyle:
Diana Munz (left), Silver; Brooke Bennett (center), Gold

9/17/00 Swimming, Men's 400m Individual Medley:
Erik Vendt (left), Silver; Tom Dolan (center), Gold

9/17/00 Swimming, Women's 100m Butterfly: Dara Torres (right), Bronze

9/17/00 Weightlifting, Women's 48kg: Tara Nott, Gold

9/18/00 Swimming, Men's 100m
Backstroke: Lenny Krayzelburg, Gold

9/18/00 Swimming, Women's 100m
Breaststroke: Megan Quann, Gold

9/19/00 Equestrian, Team Three-Day Event:(left to right) Linden
Weisman, David O'Connor, Karen O'Connor and Nina Fout, Bronze

9/19/00 Swimming, Men's 4x200m Freestyle Relay:
(left to right) Klete Keller, Jamie Rauch, Josh Davis
and Scott Goldblatt, Silver

9/19/00 Shooting, Women's Double Trap: Kimberly Rhode (right), Bronze

9/19/00 Swimming, Men's 200m Butterfly: Tom Malchow, Gold

9/19/00 Swimming, Women's 200m Individual
Medley: Christina Teuscher, Bronze

9/20/00 Archery, Men's Individual: Vic Wunderle (right), Silver

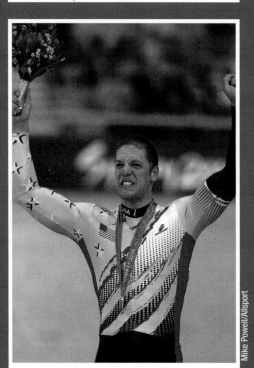

9/20/00 Cycling - Track, Sprint:
Marty Nothstein, Gold

9/20/00 Swimming, Men's 100m Freestyle:
Gary Hall Jr., Bronze

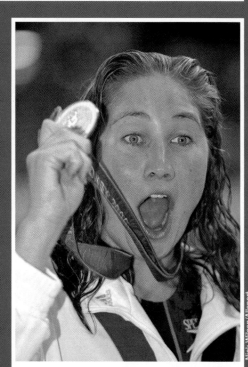

9/20/00 Swimming, Women's 200m Butterfly:
Misty Hyman, Gold

9/20/00 Swimming, Women's 4x200m Freestyle Relay: (left to right) Samantha
Arsenault, Diana Munz, Lindsay Benko and Jenny Thompson, Gold

9/21/00 Swimming, Men's 200m Backstroke:
Aaron Peirsol (left), Silver; Lenny Krayzelburg, Gold

9/21/00 Swimming, Men's 200m Individual Medley:
Tom Wilkens (left), Bronze; Tom Dolan, Silver

9/21/00 Swimming, Women's 200m Breaststroke:
Amanda Beard (left), Bronze; Kristy Kowal (right), Silver

9/21/00 Swimming, Women's 100m Freestyle:
Dara Torres (left), Bronze; Jenny Thompson, Bronze

9/22/00 Athletics, Men's Shot Put:
Adam Nelson (left), Silver; John Godina (right), Bronze

9/22/00 Equestrian, Individual Three-Day Event:
David O'Connor, Gold

9/22/00 Archery, Men's Team:
(left to right) Vic Wunderle, Rodney White and Butch Johnson, Bronze

*9/22/00 Weightlifting, Women's 75+ kg:
Cheryl Haworth, Bronze*

*9/22/00 Swimming, Men's 50m Freestyle:
Anthony Ervin (left), Gold, Gary Hall Jr., Gold*

*9/23/00 Athletics, Men's 100m:
Maurice Greene(right), Gold*

*9/22/00 Swimming, Women's 800m Freestyle:
Kaitlin Sandeno (left), Bronze; Brooke Bennett, Gold*

9/23/00 Athletics, Women's 100m: Marion Jones, Gold

9/23/00 Rowing, Women's Coxless Pair:
Karen Kraft (left), Missy Ryan, Bronze

9/23/00 Rowing, Women's Lightweight Double Sculls:
Sarah Garner (left) and Christine Collins, Bronze

9/24/00 Diving, Women's 10m Platform:
Laura Wilkinson, Gold

9/23/00 Swimming, Men's 1500m Freestyle: Chris Thompson (right), Bronze

9/23/00 Swimming, Men's 4x100m Medley:
(left to right) Ed Moses, Ian Crocker, Lenny Krayzelburg and Gary Hall Jr., Gold

9/23/00 Swimming, Women's 4x100m Medley:
Dara Torres, Jenny Thompson, Megan Quann and B. J. Bedford, Gold

9/25/00 Athletics, Men's 400m:
Alvin Harrison (left), Silver; Michael Johnson, Gold

9/25/00 Athletics, Men's 110m Hurdles:
Terrence Trammell, Silver

9/25/00 Athletics, Men's 110m Hurdles:
Mark Crear, Bronze

9/25/00 Sailing, 49er:
(left) Jonathan and Charlie McKee, Bronze

9/26/00 Volleyball, Men's Beach:
Eric Fonoimoana (left) and Dain Blanton, Gold

9/25/00 Athletics, Women's Pole Vault:
Stacy Dragila, Gold

9/26/00 Equestrian, Team Dressage:
(left to right) Guenter Seidel, Christine Traurig, Sue Blinks and Robert Dover, Bronze

9/26/00 Wrestling, Greco-Roman 97kg:
Garrett Lowney, Bronze

9/26/00 Wrestling, Greco-Roman 76kg:
Matt Lindland, Silver

9/26/00 Softball: Team USA, Gold, Christie Ambrosi, Christa Williams,
Lisa Fernandez, Leah O'Brien-Amico and Lori Harrigan (pictured left to right)

9/27/00 Athletics, Men's 400m Hurdles:
Angelo Taylor, Gold

9/27/00 Athletics, Women's 100m Hurdles:
Melissa Morrison, Bronze

JOY &
DESPAIR

Tommy Lasorda tearfully calls winning the gold medal in Olympic baseball the "greatest experience of my life."

Above: Oleksan Stepanyan of Ukraine (left) and Zetian Sheng of China plead with the referee in the men's 58kg Greco-Roman wrestling.

Below: Jose Navarro of the U.S. (left) is jubilant to get the points decision over a distraught Hicham Mesbahi of Morocco in their 51kg boxing match.

203

Tatiana Grigorieva of Australia takes the silver medal in the women's pole vault final.

British coxless pair rowers Ed Goode and Greg Searle are despondent after U.S. rowers Sebastian Bea and Matthew Long edged them out of a bronze medal by just twelve hundredths of a second.

Stu Forster/Allsport

Above: Great Britain's men's hockey team protests to the umpire during the match against Pakistan.

Al Bello/Allsport

The gold medal-winning Australian 4x100-meter freestyle relay team of Ashley Callus, Chris Fydler, Michael Klim and Ian Thorpe (left to right) celebrate.

Right: Dara Torres celebrates her gold medal win in the women's 4x100-meter medley relay.

Below: The Italian team celebrates victory as Hugues Obry of France lies on the floor in despair after the men's team epee fencing gold medal match.

Vince Carter of the U.S. men's basketball team waves to photographers while waiting to receive his gold medal.

Below: Igor Astapkovich of Belarus roars his way to bronze in men's hammer throw.

Above: A heartbroken Emi Naito of Japan shows emotion after losing the women's softball gold medal game to the U.S.

Ian Stark of Great Britain trudges out of the water after coming off his horse, Jaybee, during the cross-country section of the team three-day event.

Top left: Jane Saville of Australia is inconsolable after being disqualified as she led the race into Olympic Stadium at the end of the women's 20-kilometer walk.

Top right: Trine Hattestad of Norway celebrates after winning gold in women's javelin.

Below: Florian Kunz of Germany reflects on his team's defeat in the men's hockey preliminaries.

Sydney 2000

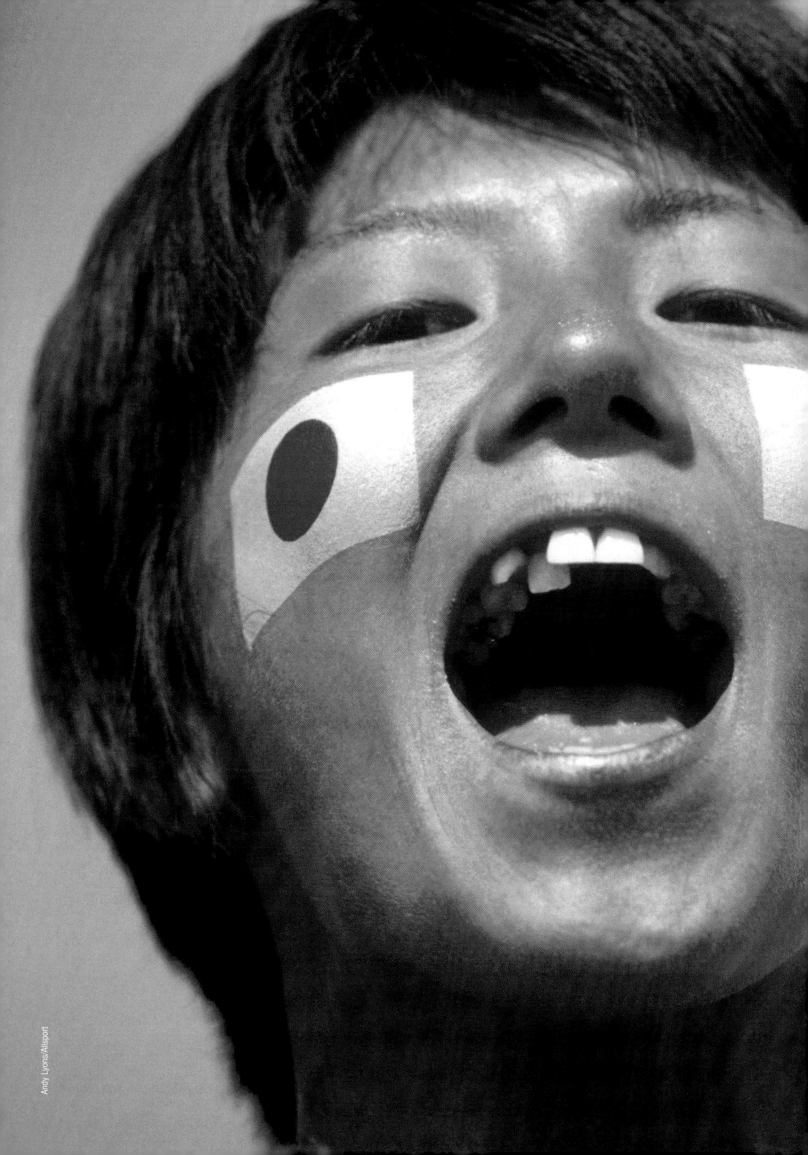

A young Japanese fan screams for her team as they battle the U.S. softball team for the gold medal.

PEOPLE

Right: U.S. soccer fans cheer for their team during the women's gold medal game.

Robert Cianflone/Allsport

Darrin Braybrook/Allsport

Left: Fans cheer the Chilean men's soccer team during their game against Cameroon. Cameroon went on to win the country's first gold medal against Spain in the finals.

Below: Australian women's water polo fans cheer their team on to a gold medal.

Darren England/Allsport

Above: A Norwegian fan cheers during the men's beach volleyball preliminaries.

Left: Fans celebrate the Italian men's volleyball team's victory over Argentina that netted Italy the bronze medal.

213

Ezra Shaw/Allsport

Above: Brazilian fans cheer the women's beach volleyball team.

Shaun Botterill/Allsport

Above: The Australian crowd watches the women's beach volleyball competition.

Gary M. Prior/Allsport

Right: A young Australian fan cheers for her country's Olympic icon, Cathy Freeman, as she receives her gold medal for the women's 400-meter race.

Korean fans cheer their women's basketball team on to a victory and fourth place standing overall.

An athletics official tries to keep dry during competition.

STARS & STRIPES

*America celebrates Sydney 2000
with pride and Old Glory*

Rulon Gardner

Women's Swimming 4x200 Team

Vince Carter

Serena and Venus Williams

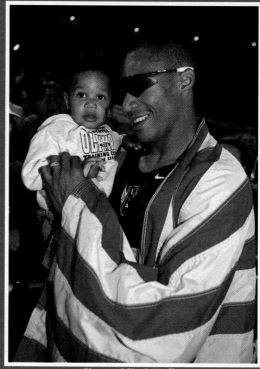
Chris and Zach Huffins

Dain Blanton

Nick Hysong

Lisa Leslie

Michael Johnson and Alvin Harrison

Team USA Baseball

Stacy Dragila

Marty Nothstein

Women's Swimming 4x100 Team

Dot Richardson

RESULTS

4	ITA	BARTOLI Michele	5: 30:34.004
5	FRA	JALABERT Laurent	5: 30:34.005
6	DEN	HOJ Frank	5: 30:34.006
7	POL	WADECKI Piotr	5: 30:34.007
8	USA	HINCAPIE George	5: 30:34.008
13	USA	ARMSTRONG Lance	5: 30:37.013
34	USA	RODRIGUEZ Fred	5: 30:46.034
49	USA	HAMILTON Tyler	5: 30:46.049
52	USA	CRUZ Antonio	5: 30:46.052

Men's Individual Time Trial

Rank	Ctry	Athlete	Time
1	RUS	EKIMOV Viacheslav	57:40.420
2	GER	ULLRICH Jan	57:48.333
3	USA	ARMSTRONG Lance	58:14.267
4	ESP	OLANO Abraham	58:31.647
5	FRA	JALABERT Laurent	58:44.455
6	KAZ	TETERIOUK Andrei	58:52.342
7	NOR	HUSHOVD Thor	59:00.015
8	ESP	GONZALEZ CAPILLA Santos	59:03.202
10	USA	HAMILTON Tyler	59:26.548

Women's Road Race

Rank	Ctry	Athlete	Time
1	NED	ZIJLAARD Leontien	3: 6:31.001
2	GER	KUPFERNAGEL Hanka	3: 6:31.002
3	LTU	ZILIUTE Diana	3: 6:31.003
4	AUS	WILSON Anna	3: 6:31.004
5	RUS	BOUBNENKOVA Svetlana	3: 6:31.005
6	FRA	le FLOC'H Magali	3: 6:31.006
7	RUS	ZABIROVA Zoulfia	3: 6:31.007
8	BEL	van de VIJVER Heidi	3: 6:31.008
47	USA	FREEDMAN Nicole	3: 28:28.047
-	USA	HOLDEN Mari	DNF
-	USA	KURRECK Karen	DNF

Women's Individual Time Trial

Rank	Ctry	Athlete	Time
1	NED	ZIJLAARD Leontien	42:00.8
2	USA	HOLDEN Mari	42:37.4
3	FRA	LONGO-CIPRELLI Jeannie	42:52.5
4	AUS	WILSON Anna	42:58.8
5	ESP	SOMARRIBA ARROLA Joane	43:06.6
6	CAN	HUGHES Clara	43:12.5
7	GER	ARNDT Judith	43:31.8
8	GER	KUPFERNAGEL Hanka	43:37.9
-	USA	KURRECK Karen	44:33

Men's 1km Time Trial

Rank	Ctry	Athlete	Time
1	GBR	QUEALLY Jason	1:01.609/OR
2	GER	NIMKE Stefan	1:02.487
3	AUS	KELLY Shane	1:02.818
4	GER	LAUSBERG Soeren	1:02.937
5	FRA	TOURNANT Arnaud	1:03.023
6	GRE	GEORGALIS Dimitrios	1:04.018
7	POL	KREJNER Grzegorz	1:04.156
8	RSA	BLOCH Garen	1:04.478
14	USA	CARNEY Jonas	1:05.968

Men's Sprint

Rank	Ctry	Athlete	Time
1	USA	NOTHSTEIN Marty	10.874
2	FRA	ROUSSEAU Florian	
3	GER	FIEDLER Jens	10.732
4	FRA	GANE Laurent	
5	GER	van EIJDEN Jan	11.040
6	ESP	VILLANUEVA Jose	
7	AUS	EADIE Sean	
8	GBR	MACLEAN Craig	
11	USA	ARRUE Marcelo	

Men's Individual Pursuit

Rank	Ctry	Athlete	Time
1	GER	BARTKO Robert	4:18.515/OR
2	GER	LEHMANN Jens	4:23.824
3	AUS	McGEE Brad	4:19.250
4	GBR	HAYLES Rob	4:19.613
5	FRA	GAUMONT Philippe	4:22.142
6	UKR	SYMONENKO Oleksandr	4:23.983
7	UKR	MATVEYEV Sergiy	4:25.380
8	ARG	PEREZ Walter Fernando	4:30.757
10	USA	FRIEDICK Mariano	4:31.241
12	USA	VANDE VELDE Christian	4:31.528
-	USA	CASEY Dylan	did not race

Men's Team Pursuit

Rank	Ctry	Athletes	Time
1	GER	BARTKO Robert/FULST Guido/ LEHMANN Jens/BECKE Daniel	3:59.710/WR
2	UKR	SYMONENKO Oleksandr/ MATVEYEV Sergiy/ FEDENKO Oleksandr/ CHERNYAVSKYY Sergiy	4:04.520
3	GBR	MANNING Paul/WIGGINS Bradley/ NEWTON Chris/STEEL Bryan	4:01.979
4	FRA	BOS Cyril/NEUVILLE Jerome/ MOREAU Francis /ERMENAULT Philippe	4:05.991
5	AUS	AITKEN Brett/ROGERS Michael/ LANCASTER Brett/BROWN Graeme	4:03.209
6	NZL	CARSWELL Tim/VERTONGEN Lee/ ANDERSON Gary/ HENDERSON Greg	4:06.495
7	NED	SCHEP Peter/SLIPPENS Robert/ MOURIS Jens/ZUIJDERWIJK Wilco	Overlapped
8	RUS	KARPETS Vladimir/ MARKOV Alexey/KLIMOV Sergey/ SMYSLOV Denis	Overlapped
12	USA	BOUCHARD-HALL Derek/ HARTWELL Erin/MULKEY Tommy/ FRIEDICK Mariano	
-	USA	CASEY Dylan/ VANDE VELDE Christian	did not race

Men's Points Race

Rank	Ctry	Athlete	Points
1	ESP	LLANERAS Juan	14
2	URU	WYNANTS Milton	18
3	RUS	MARKOV Alexey	16
4	KOR	CHO Ho-Sung	15
5	USA	CARNEY Jamie	10
6	AUT	STOCHER Franz	8
7	NZL	THOMSON Glen	6
8	ITA	MARTINELLO Silvio	5

Men's Keirin

Rank	Ctry	Athlete	Time
1	FRA	ROUSSEAU Florian	11.020
2	AUS	NEIWAND Gary	
3	GER	FIEDLER Jens	
4	GER	van EIJDEN Jan	
5	USA	NOTHSTEIN Marty	
6	FRA	MAGNE Frederic	
-	USA	ARRUE Marcelo	failed to advance

Men's Olympic Sprint

Rank	Ctry	Athletes	Time
1	FRA	GANE Laurent/TOURNANT Arnaud/ ROUSSEAU Florian	44.233
2	GBR	MACLEAN Craig/HOY Chris/ QUEALLY Jason	44.680
3	AUS	EADIE Sean/NEIWAND Gary/ HILL Darryn	45.161
4	GRE	VASILOPOULOS Lampros/ BARGKAS Kleanthis/ GEORGALIS Dimitrios	45.332
5	JAP	INAMURA Narihiro/ KAMIYAMA Yuichiro/ NAGATSUKA Tomohiro	45.264
6	SVK	BAZALIK Peter/LEPKA Jan/ JERABEK Jaroslav	45.523
7	GER	FIEDLER Jens/LAUSBERG Soeren/ NIMKE Stefan	45.537
8	LAT	BERZINS Viesturs/KIKSIS Ainars/ LAKUCS Ivo	46.525
12	USA	ARRUE Marcelo/BAIROS Johnny/ CARNEY Jonas	46.337

Men's Madison

Rank	Ctry	Athletes	Points
1	AUS	AITKEN Brett/McGRORY Scott	26
2	BEL	de WILDE Etienne/GILMORE Matthew	22
3	ITA	VILLA Marco/MARTINELLO Silvio	15
4	GBR	WIGGINS Bradley/HAYLES Rob	13
5	AUT	GARBER Roland/RIEBENBAUER Werner	10
6	GER	FULST Guido/POLLACK Olaf	9
7	ARG	CURUCHET Juan Esteban/ CURUCHET Gabriel Ovidio	9
8	NED	SLIPPENS Robert/ STAM Danny	8
		No USA entry	

Women's 500m Time Trial

Rank	Ctry	Athlete	Time
1	FRA	BALLANGER Felicia	34.140/OR
2	AUS	FERRIS Michelle	34.696
3	CHN	JIANG Cuihua	34.768
4	CHN	WANG Yan	35.013
5	USA	WITTY Chris	35.230
6	GER	WEICHELT Ulrike	35.315
7	GER	FREITAG Kathrin	35.473
8	CAN	DUBNICOFF Tanya	35.486

Women's Sprint

Rank	Ctry	Athlete	Time
1	FRA	BALLANGER Felicia	11.810
2	RUS	GRICHINA Oxana	
3	UKR	YANOVYCH Iryna	12.156
4	AUS	FERRIS Michelle	
5	HUN	SZABOLCSI Szilvia Noemi	12.426
6	USA	LINDENMUTH Tanya	
7	CAN	DUBNICOFF Tanya	
8	VEN	LARREAL Daniela	

Women's Individual Pursuit

Rank	Ctry	Athlete	Time
1	NED	ZIJLAARD Leontien	3:33.360
2	FRA	CLIGNET Marion	3:38.751
3	GBR	McGREGOR Yvonne	3:38.850
4	NZL	ULMER Sarah	3:38.930
5	ITA	BELLUTTI Antonella	3:36.967
6	GER	ARNDT Judith	3:37.609
7	AUS	BURNS Alayna	3:38.223
8	USA	VEENSTRA-MIRABELLA Erin	3:38.431

Women's Points Race

Rank	Ctry	Athlete	Points
1	ITA	BELLUTTI Antonella	19
2	NED	ZIJLAARD Leontien	16
3	RUS	SLIOUSSAREVA Olga	15
4	GER	ARNDT Judith	12
5	MEX	GUERRERO MENDEZ Belem	12
6	FRA	CLIGNET Marion	11
7	ESP	RUANO Teodora	10
8	NZL	ULMER Sarah	9
10	USA	VEENSTRA-MIRABELLA Erin	6

DIVING

Men's 3m Springboard

Rank	Ctry	Athlete	Total
1	CHN	XIONG Ni	708.72
2	MEX	PLATAS Fernando	708.42
3	RUS	SAOUTINE Dmitri	703.20
4	CHN	XIAO Hailiang	671.04
5	AUS	PULLAR Dean	647.40
6	USA	DUMAIS Troy	642.72
7	USA	RUIZ Mark	638.22
8	JPN	TERAUCHI Ken	634.47

Men's 10m Platform

Rank	Ctry	Athlete	Total
1	CHN	TIAN Liang	724.53
2	CHN	HU Jia	713.55
3	RUS	SAOUTINE Dmitri	679.26
4	CAN	DESPATIE Alexandre	652.35
5	JPN	TERAUCHI Ken	636.90
6	USA	RUIZ Mark	625.92
7	RUS	LOUKACHINE Igor	624.51
8	AUS	HELM Mathew	618.24
9	USA	PICHLER David	616.17

Men's Synchronized 3m Springboard

Rank	Ctry	Athletes	Total
1	CHN	XIAO Hailiang/XIONG Ni	365.58
2	RUS	DOBROSKOK Alexandre/ SAOUTINE Dmitri	329.97
3	AUS	NEWBERY Robert/PULLAR Dean	322.86
4	USA	DUMAIS Troy/PICHLER David	320.91
5	MEX	PLATAS Fernando/RUEDA Eduardo	317.70
6	FRA	EMPTOZ-LACOTE Gilles/ PIERRE Frederic	310.08
7	GBR	ALLY Tony/SHIPMAN Mark	296.64
8	ITA	MARCONI Nicola/MIRANDA Donald	286.38

Men's Synchronized 10m Platform

Rank	Ctry	Athletes	Total
1	RUS	LOUKACHINE Igor/SAOUTINE Dmitri	365.04
2	CHN	HU Jia/TIAN Liang	358.74
3	GER	HEMPEL Jan/MEYER Heiko	338.88
4	GBR	TAYLOR Leon/WATERFIELD Peter	335.34
5	AUS	HELM Mathew/NEWBERY Robert	333.24
6	UKR	SKRYPNIK Oleksandr/ VOLOD'KOV Roman	332.22
7	USA	PICHLER David/RUIZ Mark	321.61
8	FRA	EMPTOZ-LACOTE Gilles/ PIERRE Frederic	314.94

Women's 3m Springboard

Rank	Ctry	Athlete	Total
1	CHN	FU Mingxia	609.42
2	CHN	GUO Jingjing	597.81
3	GER	LINDNER Doerte	574.35
4	RUS	PAKHALINA Ioulia	570.42
5	SWE	LINDBERG Anna	559.17
6	RUS	ILINA Vera	555.55
7	AUS	MICHELL Chantelle	550.68
8	USA	KEIM Jenny	534.18
12	USA	DAVISON Michelle	510.48

Women's 10m Platform

Rank	Ctry	Athlete	Total
1	USA	WILKINSON Laura	543.75
2	CHN	LI Na	542.01
3	CAN	MONTMINY Anne	540.15
4	CHN	SANG Xue	513.03
5	CAN	HEYMANS Emilie	511.92
6	UKR	ZHUPINA Olena	489.00
7	AUT	RICHTER-LIBISELLER Anja	482.16
8	RUS	TIMOCHININA Svetlana	478.89
-	USA	REILING Sara	elim semis

Women's Synchronized 3m Springboard

Rank	Ctry	Athletes	Total
1	RUS	ILINA Vera/PAKHALINA Ioulia	332.64
2	CHN	FU Mingxia/GUO Jingjing	321.60
3	UKR	SOROKINA Ganna/ZHUPINA Olena	290.34
4	AUS	MICHELL Chantelle/TOURKY Loudy	283.05
5	CAN	BULMER Eryn/HARTLEY Blythe	279.00
6	MEX	ALCALA Maria Jose/LUNA Jashia	273.84
7	GER	LINDNER Doerte/ SCHMALFUSS Conny	263.76
8	SUI	MALIEV-AVIOLAT Catherine/ SCHNEIDER Jacqueline	256.20

Women's Synchronized 10m Platform

Rank	Ctry	Athletes	Total
1	CHN	LI Na/SANG Xue	345.12
2	CAN	HEYMANS Emilie/MONTMINY Anne	312.03
3	AUS	GILMORE Rebecca/TOURKY Loudy	301.50
4	AUT	REIFF Marion/RICHTER-LIBISELLER Anja	294.00
5	USA	KEIM Jenny/WILKINSON Laura	291.42
6	RUS	OLSHEVSKAYA Evgeniya/ TIMOCHININA Svetlana	288.30
7	FRA	ARBOLES-SOUCHON Odile/ DANAUX Julie	277.14
8	MEX	ALCALA Maria Jose/ALMAZAN Azul	264.30

EQUESTRIAN

Individual Dressage

Rank	Ctry	Athlete/Horse	Total
1	NED	van GRUNSVEN Anky/BONFIRE	239.18
2	GER	WERTH Isabell/GIGOLO	234.19
3	GER	SALZGEBER Ulla/ RUSTY	230.57
4	GER	CAPELLMANN Nadine/FARBENFROH	225.88
5	NED	van BAALEN Coby/FERRO	221.36
6	NED	BONTJE Ellen/SILVANO	217.59
7	DEN	JORGENSEN Lone/KENNEDY	216.90
8	USA	BLINKS Susan/ FLIM FLAM	214.65
11	USA	TRAURIG Christine/ETIENNE	208.34
23	USA	DOVER Robert/RANIER	131.02
26	USA	SEIDEL Guenter/FOLTAIRE	-

Team Dressage

Rank	Ctry	Athlete/Horse	Total
1	GER	WERTH Isabell/GIGOLO	1908
		SIMONS de RIDDER Alexandra/ CHACOMO SALZGEBER Ulla/RUSTY	1857
			1829
		CAPELLMANN Nadine/FARBENFROH	1867
		Team Total	5632
2	NED	van GRUNSVEN Anky/BONFIRE	1875
		BONTJE Ellen/SILVANO	1786
		TEEUWISSEN Arjen/GOLIATH	1831
		van BAALEN Coby/FERRO	1873
		Team Total	5579
3	USA	DOVER Robert/RANIER	1678
		BLINKS Susan/FLIM FLAM	1725
		SEIDEL Guenter/FOLTAIRE	1695
		TRAURIG Christine/ETIENNE	1746
		Team Total	5166
4	DEN	PEDERSEN Jon/ESPRIT DE VALDEMAR	1728
		THOMSEN Morten/GAY	1536
		van OLST Anne/ANY HOW	1625
		JORGENSEN Lone/KENNEDY	1796
		Team Total	5149
5	ESP	JIMENEZ Juan Antonio/GUIZO	1638
		SOTO Rafael/INVASOR	1663
		LUCIO Luis/ALJARAFE	1553
		FERRER-SALAT Beatriz/BEAUVALAIS	1710
		Team Total	5011
6	AUS	OATLEY-NIST Kristy/WALL STREET	1704
		DOWNS Rachael/APHRODITE	1613
		MACMILLAN Ricky/CRISP	1602
		HANNA Mary/LIMBO	1608
		Team Total	4925
7	SUI	BOTTANI Patricia/DIAMOND	1615
		RAMSEIER Daniel/RALI BABA	1664
		STUECKELBERGER Christine/ AQUAMARIN	1637
		CANTAMESSA Francoise/SIR S	1623
		Team Total	4924
8	GBR	FAURIE Emile/RASCHER HOPES	1674
		HESTER Carl/ARGENTILE GULLIT	1622
		MEPHAM Kirsty/DIKKILOO	1570
		DAVISON Richard/ASKARI	1602
		Team Total	4898

Individual Jumping

Rank	Ctry	Athlete/Horse	Total
1	NED	DUBBELDAM Jeroen/SJIEM	4.00
2	NED	VOORN Albert/LANDO	4.00
3	KSA	AL EID Khaled/KHASHM AL AAN	4.00
4	BRA	JOHANNPETER Andre/CALEI	8.00
4	GER	NIEBERG Lars/ESPRIT FRH	8.00
4	BEL	PHILIPPAERTS Ludo/OTTERONGO	8.00
4	GER	EHNING Marcus/FOR PLEASURE	8.00
4	GER	BECKER Otto/CENTO	8.00
10	USA	GOLDSTEIN ENGLE Margie/PERIN	12.00
15	USA	HOUGH Lauren/CLASIKO	16.00
-	USA	KRAUT Laura/LIBERTY	WDR
-	USA	GARSON Nona/Rythmical	elim

Team Jumping

Rank	Ctry	Athlete/Horse	Total
1	GER	EHNING Marcus/FOR PLEASURE	7.00
		BECKER Otto/CENTO	0.00
		NIEBERG Lars/ESPRIT FRH	8.00
		BEERBAUM Ludger/GOLDFEVER 3	36.25
		Team Total	15.00
2	SUI	McNAUGHT Lesley/DULF	23.50
		FUCHS Markus/TINKA'S BOY	8.00
		MAENDLI Beat/POZITANO	8.00
		MELLIGER Willi/CALVARO V	0.00
		Team Total	16.00
3	BRA	DE AZEVEDO Luiz Felipe/RALPH	8.00
		JOHANNPETER Andre/CALEI	24.00
		MIRANDA NETO Alvaro/ASPEN	16.00
		PESSOA Rodrigo/BALOUBET DU ROUET	0.00
		Team Total	24.00

4	FRA	LEDERMANN Alexandra/ROCHET M	0.00
		DELAVEAU Patrice/CAUCALIS	ELI
		POMEL Thierry/THOR DES CHAINES	8.00
		ROZIER Philippe/BARBARIAN	16.00
		Team Total	24.00
5	NED	VOORN Albert/LANDO	8.00
		DUBBELDAM Jeroen/SJIEM	12.00
		TOPS Jan/ROOFS	25.25
		LANSINK Jos/CARTHAGO Z	12.00
		Team Total	32.00
6	USA	KRAUT Laura/LIBERTY	12.00
		HOUGH Lauren/CLASIKO	16.00
		GARSON Nona/RHYTHMICAL	36.00
		GOLDSTEIN ENGLE Margie/PERIN	8.00
		Team Total	36.00
7	SWE	BARYARD Malin/BUTTERFLY FLIP	20.75
		BRATT Lisen/CASANOVA	16.00
		LUNDBAECK Helena/MYNTA	12.00
		GRETZER Maria/FELICIANO	20.25
		Team Total	36.75
8	GBR	WHITAKER Michael/PRINCE OF WALES	16.00
		BILLINGTON Geoff/IT'S OTTO	20.75
		EDWARDS Carl/BIT MORE CANDY	32.50
		WHITAKER John/CALVARO	4.00
		Team Total	40.50

Individual Three-Day Event

Rank	Ctry	Athlete/Horse	Total
1	USA	O'CONNOR David/CUSTOM MADE	34.00
2	AUS	HOY Andrew/SWIZZLE IN	39.80
3	NZL	TODD Mark/EYESPY II	42.00
4	FRA	SCHERER Rodolphe/BAMBI DE BRIERE	46.40
5	ITA	MAGNI Fabio/COOL'N BREEZY	49.00
6	GRE	ANTIKATZIDIS Heidi/MICHAELMAS	50.40
7	GBR	KING Mary/STAR APPEAL	52.00
8	USA	COSTELLO Robert/CHEVALIER	52.40
9	USA	BLACK Julie/HYDE PARK CORNER	53.60

Team Three-Day Event

Rank	Ctry	Athlete/Horse	Total
1	AUS	RYAN Matt/KIBAH SANDSTONE	60.20
		DUTTON Phillip/HOUSE DOCTOR	63.60
		TINNEY Stuart/JEEPSTER	41.00
		HOY Andrew/DARIEN POWERS	45.60
		Team Total	146.80
2	GBR	BRAKEWELL Jeanette/OVER TO YOU	61.60
		LAW Leslie/SHEAR H2O	54.00
		FUNNELL Pippa/SUPREME ROCK	45.40
		Team Total	161.00
3	USA	FOUT Nina/3 MAGIC BEANS	86.00
		O'CONNOR David/GILTEDGE	46.80
		O'CONNOR Karen/PRINCE PANACHE	43.00
		WIESMAN Linden/ANDEROO	ELI
		Team Total	175.80
4	GER	HAGENER Nele/LITTLE McMUFFIN	262.40
		DIBOWSKI Andreas/LEONAS DANCER	130.20
		KOEHNCKE Marina/SIR TOBY 4	70.40
		KLIMKE Ingrid/SLEEP LATE	41.20
		Team Total	241.80
5	IRL	CASSIDY Nicola/MR MULLINS	124.20
		McGRATH Virgina/THE YELLOW EARL	139.60
		SHORTT Susan/JOY OF MY HEART	80.00
		DONEGAN Patricia/DON'T STEP BACK	65.80
		Team Total	270.00
6	BRA	FOFANOFF Serguei/SANDERSTON	216.20
		ARAUJO NETO Vicente/TEVERI	124.80
		PAGOTO Eder/ AMAZONIAN DO FEROLETO	128.80
		FARIA Luiz Augusto/HUNEFER	79.40
		Team Total	333.00
7	ESP	BECA Ramon/PERSEUS II	176.40
		SARASOLA Enrique/SUPER DJARVIS	164.80
		Team Total	1341.20
8	NZL	TODD Mark/DIAMOND HALL RED	65.60
		JEFFERIS Vaughn/BOUNCE	WDR
		Team Total	2065.60

FENCING

Men's Individual Foil

Rank	Ctry	Athlete
1	KOR	KIM Young-Ho
2	GER	BISSDORF Ralf
3	RUS	CHEVTCHENKO Dmitri
4	FRA	FERRARI Jean-Noel
5	ITA	SANZO Salvatore
6	UKR	GOLUBYTSKY Sergiy
7	GER	BREUTNER Richard
8	HUN	MARSI Mark
10	USA	BAYER Cliff

Men's Team Foil

Rank	Ctry	Athletes
1	FRA	FERRARI Jean-Noel/GUYART Brice/ L'HOTELLIER Patrice/PLUMENAIL Lionel
2	CHN	DONG Zhaozhi/WANG Haibin/ YE Chong/ZHANG Jie
3	ITA	CROSTA Daniele/MAGNI Gabriele/ SANZO Salvatore/ZENNARO Matteo
4	POL	KIELPIKOWSKI Piotr/KRZESINSKI Adam/ MOCEK Slawomir/SOBCZAK Ryszard
5	UKR	BRYZGALOV Oleksii/GOLUBYTSKY Sergiy/ GORBACHUK Oleksandr/KRUGLYAK Oleksiy
6	GER	BISSDORF Ralf/BREUTNER Richard/ HAUSMANN David/WIENAND Wolfgang
7	CUB	GARCIA Oscar/GREGORY Elvis/

| 8 | RUS | TREVEJO Ivan/TUCKER Rolando CHEVTCHENKO Dmitri/DEEV Andrey/ LAKATOSH Alexander/MAMEDOV Ilgar |
| | | No USA entry |

Men's Individual Sabre

Rank	Ctry	Athlete
1	ROM	COVALIU Mihai Claudiu
2	FRA	GOURDAIN Mathieu
3	GER	KOTHNY Wiradech
4	HUN	FERJANCSIK Domonkos
5	FRA	TOUYA Damien
6	RUS	FROSSINE Alexei
7	ITA	TERENZI Tonhi
8	ROM	GAUREANU Victor Dan
30	USA	SMART Keeth
34	USA	SPENCER-EL Akhnaten

Men's Team Sabre

Rank	Ctry	Athletes
1	RUS	CHARIKOV Serguei/DYACHENKO Alexey/ FROSSINE Alexei/POZDNIAKOV Stanislav
2	FRA	GOURDAIN Mathieu/PILLET Julien/ SEGUIN Cedric/TOUYA Damien
3	GER	BAUER Dennis/KOTHNY Wiradech/ LEHMANN Eero/WEBER Alexander
4	ROM	COVALIU Mihai Claudiu/ GAUREANU Victor Dan/ LUPEICA Florin Alin/SANDU Constantin
5	HUN	FERJANCSIK Domonkos/KOVES Csaba/ NEMCSIK Zsolt/TAKACS Peter
6	UKR	HUTTSAIT Vadym/KALYUZHNYY Volodymyr/ LUKASHENKO Volodymyr
7	POL	JASKOT Norbert/SOBALA Marcin/ STUSINSKI Tomasz/SZNAJDER Rafal
8	ITA	CASERTA Raffaello/PASTORE Giampero/ TARANTINO Luigi/TERENZI Tonhi
		No USA entry

Men's Individual Epee

Rank	Ctry	Athlete
1	RUS	KOLOBKOV Pavel
2	FRA	OBRY Hugues
3	KOR	LEE Sang-Ki
4	SUI	FISCHER Marcel
5	SWE	VANKY Peter
6	CUB	TREVEJO Ivan
7	FRA	SRECKI Eric
8	CHN	ZHAO Gang
29	USA	BLOOM Tamir

Men's Team Epee

Rank	Ctry	Athletes
1	ITA	MAZZONI Angelo/MILANOLI Paolo/ RANDAZZO Maurizio/ROTA Alfredo
2	FRA	di MARTINO Jean FranÂois/LEROUX Robert/ OBRY Hugues/SRECKI Eric
3	CUB	LOYOLA Nelson/MAYA Candido Alberto/ PEDROSO Carlos/TREVEJO Ivan
4	KOR	KU Kyo-Dong/LEE Sang-Ki/ LEE Sang-Yup/YANG Roy-Sung
5	GER	FIEDLER Joerg/SCHMITT Arnd/ STEIFENSAND Marc/STRIGEL Daniel
6	BLR	MURASHKO Andrei/PCHENIKIN Vladimir/ RASOLKO Sergei/ZAKHAROV Vitaly
7	HUN	FEKETE Attila/KOVACS Ivan/ MARSI Mark
8	AUS	ADAMS Gerard/CARTILLIER Luc/ HEFFERNAN Nick
		No USA entry

Women's Individual Foil

Rank	Ctry	Athlete
1	ITA	VEZZALI Valentina
2	GER	KOENIG Rita
3	ITA	TRILLINI Giovanna
4	ROM	CARLESCU BADEA Laura Gabriela
5	CHN	XIAO Aihua
6	ITA	BIANCHEDI Diana
7	HUN	MOHAMED Aida
8	ROM	SZABO Reka Zsofia
11	USA	ZIMMERMANN Iris
16	USA	MARSH Ann
20	USA	ZIMMERMANN Felicia

Women's Team Foil

Rank	Ctry	Athletes
1	ITA	BIANCHEDI Diana/GIACOMETTI Annamaria/ TRILLINI Giovanna/VEZZALI Valentina
2	POL	BRUCHALA Sylwia/ MROCZKIEWICZ Magdalena/ RYBICKA Anna/WOLNICKA Barbara
3	GER	BAU Sabine/KOENIG Rita/ SCHIEL Gesine/WEBER Monika
4	USA	MARSH Ann/SMART Erinn/ ZIMMERMANN Felicia/ZIMMERMANN Iris
5	RUS	BOIKO Svetlana/CHARKOVA Olga/ IOUCHEVA Ekaterina/NUSUEVA Bela
6	HUN	KNAPEK Edina/LANTOS Gabriella/ MOHAMED Aida/VARGA Katalin
7	CHN	MENG Jie/XIAO Aihua/ YUAN Li/ZHANG Lei
8	UKR	KOLTSOVA Olena/ LELEYKO Olga Oleksandrivna/ VASYLYEVA Lyudmyla

Women

Rank	Cntry	Record
1	AUS	4-3
2	USA	4-2-1(final)
3	RUS	4-3
4	NED	(3rd-4th)
5	CAN	
6	KAZ	

USA MATCH SCORES: USA vs NED - 6-4; USA vs CAN - 8-8; USA vs RUS - 7-5; USA vs AUS - 6-7; USA vs KAZ - 9-6; USA vs NED - 6-5; USA vs AUS - 3-4

USA TEAM: BEAUREGARD Robin/ESTES Ellen/JOHNSON Courtney/LORENZ Ericka/MOODY Heather/ORWIG Bernice/O'TOOLE Maureen/PAYNE Nicolle/PETRI Heather/SHEEHY Kathy/SIMMONS Coralie/SWAIL Julie/VILLA Brenda/Head Coach: BAKER Guy William/Second Coach: LINDGREN Kenneth Edward/Assitant Coach: DUPLANTY Christopher David

WEIGHTLIFTING

Men's 56 kg

Rank/Ctry/Athlete		Snatch	C&J	Total
1	TUR	MUTLU Halil	137.5 WR	167.5 WR	305.0 WR
2	CHN	WU Wenxiong	125.0	162.5	287.5
3	CHN	ZHANG Xiangxiang	125.0	162.5	287.5
4	TPE	WANG Shin-Yuan	125.0	160.0	285.0
5	CUB	ALVAREZ Sergio	120.0	155.0	275.0
6	ROM	JIGAU Adrian Ioan	122.5	152.5	275.0
7	BLR	DERBENEV Vitaly	125.0	150.0	275.0
8	TPE	YANG Chin-Yi	120.0	150.0	270.0
		No USA entry			

Men's 62 kg

Rank/Ctry/Athlete		Snatch	C&J	Total
1	CRO	PECHALOV Nikolay	150.0/OR	175.0	325.0/OR
2	GRE	SABANIS Leonidas	147.5/OR	170.0	317.5
3	BLR	OLESHCHUK Gennady	142.5	175.0	317.5
4	CHN	LE Maosheng	140.0	175.0	315.0
5	IRI	PANZVAN LANGROUDI Seyed Mahdi	140.0	162.5	302.5
6	JPN	IKEHATA Hiroshi	135.0	165.0	300.0
7	MDA	POPOV Vladimir	135.0	160.0	295.0
8	AZE	SULEYMANOV Elkhan	130.0	162.5	292.5
		No USA entry			

Men's 69 kg

Rank/Ctry/Athlete		Snatch	C&J	Total
1	BUL	BOEVSKI Galabin	162.5	195.0/WR	357.5/OR
2	BUL	MARKOV Georgi	165.0/WR	187.5	352.5
3	BLR	LAVRENOV Sergei	157.5	182.5	340.0
4	CHN	ZHANG Guozheng	152.5	185.0	337.5
5	ARM	PETROSYAN Rudik	147.5	187.5	335.0
6	GRE	LEONIDIS Valerios	145.0	185.0	330.0
7	KOR	LEE Bae-Young	142.5	187.5	330.0
8	KOR	KIM Hak-Bong	147.5	182.5	330.0
		No USA entry			

Men's 77 kg

Rank/Ctry/Athlete		Snatch	C&J	Total
1	CHN	ZHAN Xugang	160.0	207.5/OR	367.5
2	GRE	MITROU Viktor	165.0	202.5	367.5
3	ARM	MELIKYAN Arsen	167.5	197.5	365.0
4	KAZ	FILIMONOV Sergey	167.5	195.0	362.5
5	ALB	SULI Ilirian	162.5	192.5	355.0
6	PRK	JON Chol Ho	162.5	190.0	352.5
7	GER	STEINHOEFEL Ingo	160.0	190.0	350.0
8	UKR	HNIDENKO Dmytro	160.0	190.0	350.0
12	USA	CHAPLIN III Oscar	155.0	180.0	335.0

Men's 85 kg

Rank/Ctry/Athlete		Snatch	C&J	Total
1	GRE	DIMAS Pyrros	175.0	215.0	390.0
2	GER	HUSTER Marc	177.5	212.5	390.0
3	GEO	ASANIDZE George	180.0	210.0	390.0
4	POL	SIEMION Krzysztof	167.5	212.5	380.0
5	ARM	KHACHATRYAN Gagik	175.0	205.0	380.0
6	AUS	CHAKHOYAN Sergo	175.0	202.5	377.5
7	GRE	SPYROU Christos	170.0	205.0	375.0
8	CUB	QUIROGA Ernesto	165.0	210.0	375.0
		No USA entry			

Men's 94 kg

Rank/Ctry/Athlete		Snatch	C&J	Total
1	GRE	KAKIASVILIS Akakios	185.0	220.0	405.0
2	POL	KOLECKI Szymon	182.5	222.5	405.0
3	RUS	PETROV Alexei	180.0	222.5	402.5
4	IRI	BAGHERI Kouroush	187.5	215.0	402.5
5	MDA	VACARCIUC Vadim	177.5	220.0	397.5
6	HUN	KOVACS Zoltan	180.0	217.5	397.5
7	TUR	SUDAS Bunyami	177.5	215.0	392.5
8	VEN	LUNA FERMIN Julio	177.5	215.0	392.5

Men's 105 kg

Rank/Ctry/Athlete		Snatch	C&J	Total
1	IRI	TAVAKOLI Hossein	190.0	235.0	425.0
2	BUL	TSAGAEV Alan	187.5	235.0	422.5
3	QAT	ASAAD Said S	190.0	230.0	420.0
4	UKR	RAZORYONOV Igor	192.5	227.5	420.0
5	RUS	TCHIGUICHEV	190.0	225.0	415.0

7	ROM	VLAD Florin	180.0	225.0	405.0
8	POL	KLESZCZ Grzegorz	185.0	220.0	405.0
		No USA entry			

Men's 105+ kg

Rank/Ctry/Athlete		Snatch	C&J	Total
1	IRI	REZAZADEH Hossein	212.5/WR	260.0	472.5/WR
2	GER	WELLER Ronny	210.0/WR	257.5	467.5
3	RUS	CHEMERKIN Andrei	202.5	260.0	462.5
4	QAT	SALEM Jaber S	205.0	255.0	460.0
5	KOR	KIM Tae-Hyun	200.0	260.0	460.0
6	LAT	SCERBATIHS Viktors	202.5	250.0	452.5
7	POL	NAJDEK Pawel	185.0	240.0	425.0
8	HUN	STARK Tibor	195.0	230.0	425.0
10	USA	HAMMAN Shane	195.0	225.0	420.0

Women's 48 kg

Rank/Ctry/Athlete		Snatch	C&J	Total
1	USA	NOTT Tara	82.5	102.5	185.0
2	INA	RUMBEWAS Raema Lisa	80.0	105.0	185.0
3	INA	INDRIYANI Sri	82.5	100.0	182.5
4	MYA	WIN Kay Thi	80.0	100.0	180.0
5	USA	GOAD Robin	77.5	100.0	177.5
6	JPN	NIYANAGI Kaori	75.0	100.0	175.0
7	ITA	GIGANTI Eva	77.5	92.5	170.0
8	FRA	RICHARD Sabryna	70.0	87.5	157.5

Women's 53 kg

Rank/Ctry/Athlete		Snatch	C&J	Total
1	CHN	YANG Xia	100.0/WR	125.0/WR	225.0/WR
2	TPE	LI Feng-Ying	97.5/WR	115.0	212.5
3	INA	SLAMET Winarni Binti	90.0	112.5	202.5
4	NGR	GBODO Franca	85.0	110.0	195.0
5	MYA	WIN Swe Swe	85.0	110.0	195.0
6	IND	CHANU Thing Baijan Sanamacha	85.0	110.0	195.0
7	JPN	NAKAGA Mari	77.5	105.0	182.5
8	ROM	MUNTEANU Marioara	82.5	97.5	180.0
		No USA entry			

Women's 58 kg

Rank/Ctry/Athlete		Snatch	C&J	Total
1	MEX	JIMENEZ MENDIVIL Soraya	95.0	127.5	222.5
2	PRK	RI Song Hui	97.5	122.5	220.0
3	THA	SUTA Khassaraporn	92.5	117.5	210.0
4	CAN	TURCOTTE Maryse	90.0	115.0	205.0
5	POL	KLEJNOWSKA Aleksandra	90.0	112.5	202.5
7	UKR	SKAKUN Nataliya	85.0	112.5	197.5
8	BLR	BATSIUSHKO Anna	90.0	107.5	197.5
		No USA entry			

Women's 63 kg

Rank/Ctry/Athlete		Snatch	C&J	Total
1	CHN	CHEN Xiaomin	112.5 WR	130.0	242.5 WR
2	RUS	POPOVA Valentina	107.5	127.5	235.0
3	GRE	CHATZIIOANNOU Ioanna	97.5	125.0	222.5
4	THA	DETSAENG Saipin	102.5	120.0	222.5
5	PRK	KIM Yong Ok	90.0	115.0	205.0
6	AUS	PHILLIPS Amanda	82.5	107.5	190.0
7	ESP	PEREZ Josefa	85.0	102.5	187.5
8	ARG	KOPPEL Nora	80.0	102.5	182.5
		No USA entry			

Women's 69 kg

Rank/Ctry/Athlete		Snatch	C&J	Total
1	CHN	LIN Weining	110.0	132.5	242.5
2	HUN	MARKUS Erzsebet	112.5/WR	130.0	242.5
3	IND	MALLESWARI Karnam	110.0	130.0	240.0
4	BUL	TRENDAFILOVA Milena	100.0	132.5	232.5
5	BUL	KERKELOVA Daniela	100.0	132.5	232.5
6	RUS	KASSIMOVA Irina	100.0	130.0	230.0
7	THA	THONGSUK Pawina	100.0	125.0	225.0
8	POL	PREI Beata	100.0	125.0	225.0
		No USA entry			

Women's 75 kg

Rank/Ctry/Athlete		Snatch	C&J	Total
1	COL	URRUTIA Maria Isabel	110.0	135.0	245.0
2	NGR	OGBEIFO Ruth	105.0	140.0	245.0
3	TPE	KUO Yi-Hang	107.5	137.5	245.0
4	KOR	KIM Soon-Hee	105.0	135.0	240.0
5	HUN	LIKERECZ Gyongyi	105.0	122.5	227.5
6	RUS	KHABIROVA Svetlana	102.5	125.0	227.5
7	USA	HEADS-LANE Cara	102.5	120.0	222.5
8	DOM	RIJO Wanda	95.0	120.0	215.0

Women's 75+ kg

Rank/Ctry/Athlete		Snatch	C&J	Total
1	CHN	DING Meiyuan	135.0/WR	165.0/WR	300.0/WR
2	POL	WROBEL Agata	132.5/OR	162.5/OR	295.0
3	USA	HAWORTH Cheryl	125.0	145.0	270.0

4	COL	DELGADO Carmenza	115.0	145.0	260.0
5	NGR	IDAHOSA Helen	110.0	140.0	250.0
6	GER	RIESERER Monique	112.5	132.5	245.0
7	KOR	MUN Kyung-Ae	110.0	135.0	245.0
8	NZL	BAKER Olivia	105.0	130.0	235.0

WRESTLING

Men's Freestyle 54kg

Rank	Ctry	Athlete
1	AZE	ABDULLAYEV Naming
2	USA	HENSON Samuel
3	GRE	KARNTANOV Amiran
4	BLR	KONTOEV German
5	UKR	ZAKHARUK Oleksandr
6	KAZ	MAMYROV Maulen
7	MDA	RAILEAN Vitalie
8	UZB	ACHILOV Adkhamjon

Men's Freestyle 58kg

Rank	Ctry	Athlete
1	IRI	DABIR Alireza
2	UKR	BUSLOVYCH Yevgen
3	USA	BRANDS Terry
4	UZB	ZAKHARTDINOV Damir
5	MGL	PUREVBAATAR Oyunbileg
6	GEO	POGOSIAN David
7	ARM	BERBERYAN Martin
8	RUS	RAMAZANOV Murad

Men's Freestyle 63kg

Rank	Ctry	Athlete
1	RUS	OUMAKHANOV Mourad
2	BUL	BARZAKOV Serafim
3	KOR	JANG Jae Sung
4	IRI	TALAEI Mohammad
5	ARM	HAYRAPETYAN Arshak
6	CUB	ORTIZ Carlos
7	AZE	AFANDIYEV Shamil
8	SVK	FERNYAK Stefan
9	USA	KOLAT Cary

Men's Freestyle 69kg

Rank	Ctry	Athlete
1	CAN	IGALI Daniel
2	RUS	GITINOV Arsen
3	USA	McILRAVY Lincoln
4	BLR	DEMCHENKO Sergei
5	CUB	SANCHEZ Yosmany
6	MDA	DIACONU Ivan
7	ARM	GEVORGYAN Arayik
8	KGZ	ASKAROV Almaz

Men's Freestyle 76kg

Rank	Ctry	Athlete
1	USA	SLAY Brandon
2	KOR	MOON Eui Jae
3	TUR	BEREKET Adem
4	KAZ	LALIYEV Gennadiy
5	UZB	HINCHAGOV Rusian
6	AKR	MUZAYEV Alik
7	MKD	GADZIHANOV Nasir
8	POL	JURECKI Marcin

Men's Freestyle 85kg

Rank	Ctry	Athlete
1	RUS	SAITIEV Adam
2	CUB	ROMERO Yoel
3	MKD	IBRAGIMOV Mogamed
4	IRI	KHADEM AZGHADI Amirreza
5	USA	BURTON Charles
6	KOR	YANG Hyun Mo
7	HUN	KAPUVARI Gabor
8	ROM	GHITA Nicolae

Men's Freestyle 97kg

Rank	Ctry	Athlete
1	RUS	MOURTASALIYEV Saghid
2	KAZ	BAIRAMUKOV Isalm
3	GEO	KURTANIDZE Eldar
4	POL	GARMULEWICZ Marek
5	GRE	XANTHOPOULOS Aftandil
6	IRI	HEIDARI Alireza
7	BLR	SHEMAROV Aleksandr
8	NED	TORCHINAVA George
18	USA	DOUGLAS Melvin

Men's Freestyle 130kg

Rank	Ctry	Athlete
1	RUS	MOUSSOULBES David
2	UZB	TAYMAZOV Artur
3	CUB	RODRIGUEZ Alexis
4	IRI	JADIDI Abbas
5	USA	MCCOY Kerry
6	BLR	MADVEDEV Aleksei
7	GER	THIELE Sven
8	KGZ	KOWALEWSKI Alexander

Men's Greco-Roman 54kg

Rank	Ctry	Athlete
1	KOR	SIM Kwo Ho
2	CUB	RIVAS Lazaro
3	PRK	KANG Yong Gyun
4	UKR	KALASHNIKOV Andriy
5	GER	TER-MKRTCHYAN Alfred
6	CHN	WANG Hui
7	AZE	EYVAZOV Natig
8	KGZ	KALILOV Uran
17	**USA**	**MAYS Steven**

Men's Greco-Roman 58kg

Rank	Ctry	Athlete
1	BUL	NAZARIAN Armen
2	KOR	KIM In-Sub
3	CHN	SHENG Zetian
4	GER	YIDIZ Rifat
5	IRI	ASHKANI Ali
6	**USA**	**GRUENWALD James**
7	RUS	NIKONOROV Valeri
8	JPN	SASAMOTO Makoto

Men's Greco-Roman 63kg

Rank	Ctry	Athlete
1	RUS	SAMOURGACHEV Varteres
2	CUB	MAREN Juan Luis
3	GEO	CHACHUA Akaki
4	SUI	MOTZER Beat
5	UZB	KURBANOV Bakhodir
6	**USA**	**BRACKEN Kevin**
7	KAZ	MANUKYAN Mkkhitar
8	UKR	KOMYSHENKO Grygoriy

Men's Greco-Roman 69kg

Rank	Ctry	Athlete
1	CUB	AZCUY Filiberto
2	JPN	NAGATA Katsuhiko
3	RUS	GLOUCHKOV Alexei
4	EST	NIKITIN Valeri
5	KOR	SON Sang-Pil
6	AZE	DUGUCHIYEV Islam
7	POL	WOLNY Ryszard
8	UKR	ROUSTAM Adji
12	**USA**	**SIMS Heath**

Men's Greco-Roman 76kg

Rank	Ctry	Athlete
1	RUS	KARDANOV Mourat
2	**USA**	**LINDLAND Matt James**
3	FIN	YLI-HANNUKSELA Marko
4	UKR	MANUKYAN David
5	KOR	KIM Jin Soo
6	SWE	ABRAHAMIAN Ara
7	BLR	MAKARENKO Vyacheslav
8	GEO	MELELASHVLI Tarieli

Men's Greco-Roman 85kg

Rank	Ctry	Athlete
1	TUR	YERLIKAYA Hamza
2	HUN	BARDOSI Sandor Istvan
3	GEO	VAKHTANGADZE Mukhran
4	NOR	AANES Fritz
5	BLR	TSILENT Valery
6	CUB	MENDEZ Luis Enrique
7	ISR	TSITSIASHVILI Gotcha
8	SWE	LIDBERG Martin
19	**USA**	**CLARK Quincey**

Men's Greco-Roman 97kg

Rank	Ctry	Athlete
1	SWE	LJUNGBERG Mikael
2	UKR	SALDADZE Davyd
3	**USA**	**LOWNEY Garrett**
4	GRE	THANOS Konstantinos
5	GEO	CHKHAIDZE Genadi
6	KAZ	MATVIYENKO Sergey
7	SUI	BUERGLER Urs
8	LTU	EZERSKIS Mindaugas

Men's Greco-Roman 130kg

Rank	Ctry	Athlete
1	**USA**	**GARDNER Rulon**
2	RUS	KARELIN Alexandre
3	BLR	DEBELKA Dmitry
4	ISR	YEVSEYCHYC Juri
5	CUB	MILIAN Hector
6	UKR	SALDADZE Georgiy
7	ITA	GIUNTA Giuseppe
8	TUR	BAKIR Fatih

Team Roster

2000 U.S. Olympic Team Roster

ARCHERY

Women (3)

Name, Birth date, Birthplace, Hometown, Current Residence

Janet Dykman, 1/17/54, Monterey Park, CA, El Monte, CA, El Monte, CA; **Denise Parker**, 12/12/73, Salt Lake City, UT, Salt Lake City, UT, Salt Lake City, UT; **Karen Scavotto**, 4/17/82, Danbury, CT, Enfield, CT, Enfield, CT

Men (3)

Name, Birth date, Birthplace, Hometown, Current Residence

Richard (Butch) Johnson, 8/30/55, Worcester, MA, Woodstock, CT, Woodstock, CT; **Rod White**, 3/1/77, Sharon, PA, Hermitage, PA, Mnt Pleasant, IA; **Victor (Vic) Wunderle**, 3/4/76, Lincoln, IL, Mason City, IL, Mason City, IL

Team Leader: Teresa Costello, 4/10/53, Montezuma, GA, Milford, OH, Milford, OH

Men's Coach: Lloyd Brown, 3/1/61, San Diego, CA, San Diego, CA, San Diego, CA

Women's Coach: Nancy Myrick, 2/1/33, Irwin, PA, Mesa, AZ, Mesa, AZ

ATHLETICS

Women (56)

Name, Birth date, Birthplace, Hometown, Current Residence

Amy Acuff, 7/14/75, Port Arthur, TX, Corpus Christi, TX, Los Angeles, CA; **Erin Aldrich**, 12/27/77, Dallas, TX, Dallas, TX, Austin, TX; **Andrea Anderson**, 2/28/71, Harbor City, CA, Long Beach, CA, Long Beach, CA; **Mikele (Miki) Barber**, 10/4/80, Livingston, NJ, Montclair, NJ, Montclair, NJ; **Kim Batten**, 3/29/69, McRae, GA, Rochester, NY, Tallahassee, FL; **Kelly Blair-LaBounty**, 11/24/70, Prosser, WA, Prosser, WA, Austin, TX; **Lynda Blutreich**, 12/13/71, Lynn, MA, Chapel Hill, NC, Chapel Hill, NC; **Tonja Buford-Bailey**, 12/13/70, Dayton, OH, Dayton, OH, Dallas, TX; **Dawn Burrell**, 11/1/73, Philadelphia, PA, Lansdowne, PA, Houston, TX; **Shelia Burrell**, 1/15/72, Albuquerque, NM, Albuquerque, NM, Los Angeles, CA; **Yeuling Chen**, 2/4/73, Liyoning, China, San Diego, CA; **Christine Clark**, 10/10/62, n/a, Anchorage, AK, Anchorage, AK; **Hazel Clark**, 10/3/77, Livingston, NJ, Maplewood, NJ, Gainesville, FL; **Joetta Clark-Diggs**, 8/1/62, East Orange, NJ, Maplewood, NJ, Gainesville, FL; **LaTasha Colander-Richardson**, 8/23/76, Portsmouth, VA, Portsmouth, VA, Angier, NC; **Michele Collins**, 2/12/71, Canal Zone, Panama, Garland, TX, Raleigh, NC; **Sharon Couch**, 9/13/69, Richmond, VA, Stone Mountain, GA, Stone Mountain, GA; **Jesseca Cross**, 5/10/75, New Orleans, LA, Laramie, WY, Laramie, WY; **Shayne Culpepper**, 12/3/73, Atlanta, GA, Atlanta, GA, Boulder, CO; **Karol Damon**, 12/20/69, Bergstrom AFB, TX, Kansas City, MO, Kansas City, MO; **Gail Devers**, 11/19/66, Seattle, WA, Alpharetta, GA, Alpharetta, GA; **Stacy Dragila**, 3/25/71, Auburn, CA, Auburn, CA, Pocatello, ID; **Deena Drossin**, 2/14/73, Waltham, MA, Alamosa, CO,, Alamosa, CO; **Elva Dryer**, 9/26/71, Durango, CO, Durango, CO, Albuquerque, NM; **Torri Edwards**, 1/31/77, Fontana, CA, Los Angeles, CA, Los Angeles, CA; **Dawn Ellerbe**, 4/3/74, Brooklyn, NY, Laramie, WY, Laramie, WY; **Suzy Favor Hamilton**, 8/8/68, Stevens Point, WI, Madison, WI, Madison, WI; **Chryste Gaines**, 9/14/70, Lawton, OK, San Leandro, CA, San Leandro, CA; **Nicole Gamble**, 6/21/77, Sumter, SC, Sumter, SC, Sumter, SC; **Sandra Glover**, 12/30/68, Palestine, TX, Palestine, TX, Houston, TX; **Monique Henderson**, 2/18/83, San Diego, CA, Bonita, CA, Bonita, CA; **Monique Hennagan**, 5/26/76, Columbia, SC, Columbia, SC, Cola, SC; **Libbie Hickman**, 2/17/65, Billings, MT, Fort Collins, CO, Fort Collins, CO; **Marion Jones**, 10/12/75, Los Angeles, CA, Los Angeles, CA, Raleigh, NC; **Shakedia Jones**, 3/15/79, Waukegan, IL, Spring Valley, CA, Spring Valley, CA; **Kristin Kuehl**, 7/30/70, Windom, MN, Minneapolis, MN, Minneapolis, MN; **Anne Marie Lauck**, 3/7/69, Rochester, NY, Hampton, NJ, Hampton, NJ; **Debbi Lawrence**, 10/15/61, Columbus, IN, Kenosha, WI, Kenosha, WI; **Jearl Miles-Clark**, 9/4/66, Gainesville, FL, Gainesville, FL, Gainesville, FL; **Inger Miller**, 6/12/72, Los Angeles, CA, Van Nuys, CA, Van Nuys, CA; **Melissa Morrison**, 7/9/71, Mooresville, NC, Kannapolis, NC, Columbia, SC; **Melissa Mueller**, 11/16/72, Waukesha, WI, McFarland, WI, Phoenix, AZ; **DeDee Nathan**, 4/20/68, Birmingham, AL, Fort Wayne, IN, Bloomington, IN; **Amy Palmer**, 4/20/75, Tooele, UT, Grantsville, UT, Grantsville, UT; **Nanceen Perry**, 8/19/77, Fairfield, TX, Fairfield, TX, Austin, TX; **Suzy Powell**, 9/3/76, Modesto, CA, Modesto, CA, Modesto, CA; **Connie Price-Smith**, 6/3/62, St Charles, MO, St Charles, MO, Hilliard, OH; **Jen Rhines**, 7/1/74, Syracuse, NY, Liverpool, NY, Haverford, PA; **Passion Richardson**, 1/25/75, Fort Bragg, NC, Kansas City, KS, Kansas City, KS; **Michelle Rohl**, 11/12/65, Madison, WI, Black River Falls, WI, Black River Falls, WI; **Amy Rudolph**, 9/18/73, Ridgeway, PA, Warwick, RI, Warwick, RI; **Marla Runyan**, 1/4/69, Santa Maria, CA, Eugene, OR, Eugene, OR; **Seilala Sua**, 2/25/78, Fort Lauderdale, FL, Fort Lauderdale, FL, Los Angeles, CA; **Kellie Suttle**, 5/9/73, St Peters, MO, St Charles, MO, Jonesboro, AR; **Teri Tunks**, 10/30/75, Crete, NE, Dallas, TX, Dallas, TX; **Shana Williams**, 4/7/72, Bridgeton, NJ, Bridgeton, NJ, Montclair, NJ

Team Leader: Mamie Rallins, 7/8/41, Chicago, IL, Hampton, VA, Hampton, VA

Asst Team Leader: Judy Harrison, 3/30/52, Evanston, IL, Houston, TX, Houston, TX

Head Coach: Karen Dennis, 6/14/49, Detroit, MI, Las Vegas, NV, Las Vegas, NV

Asst Coach: Sandy Fowler, 6/9/59, Boston, MA, Northport, AL, Northport, AL

Asst Coach: Ernest Gregoire, 1/27/36, Plaquemine, LA, Walnut, CA, Walnut, CA

Asst Coach: Rita Somerlot, 6/7/49, Kenton, OH, Centerville, OH, Centerville, OH

Asst Coach: P LaVerne Sweat, 10/5/37, Norfolk, VA, Hampton, VA, Hampton, VA

Asst Coach: Mark Young, 5/8/46, Ann Arbor, MI, Topsfield, MA, Topsfield, MA

Men (67)

Name, Birth date, Birthplace, Hometown, Current Residence

Abdihakim (Abdi) Abdirahman, 12/2/78, Somalia, Tucson, AZ, Tucson, AZ; **Charles Austin**, 12/19/67, Bay City, TX, Bay City, TX, San Marcos, TX; **Andy Bloom**, 8/11/73, Stamford, CT, Schenectady, NY, Knoxville, TN; **Kenneth Brokenburr**, 10/29/68, Winter Haven, FL, Auburndale, FL, Raleigh, NC; **John Capel**, 11/27/78, Brooksville, FL, Brooksville, FL, Gainesville, FL; **James Carter**, 7/5/78, Baltimore, MD, Baltimore, MD, Baltimore, MD; **LaMark Carter**, 8/23/70, Shreveport, LA, Shreveport, LA, Shreveport, LA; **Curt Clausen**, 10/9/67, Trenton, NJ, Stevens Point, WI, Chula Vista, CA; **Tony Cosey**, 10/5/74, Knoxville, TN, Knoxville, TN, Knoxville, TN; **Mark Crear**, 10/2/68, San Francisco, CA, Los Angeles, CA, Valencia, CA; **Mark Croghan**, 1/8/68, Akron, OH, Greensburg, OH, Wadsworth, OH; **Alan Culpepper**, 9/15/72, Fort Worth, TX, Fort Worth, TX, Boulder, CO; **Walter Davis**, 7/2/79, Lafayette, LA, Leonville, LA, Great Bend, KS; **Lance Deal**, 8/21/61, Riverton, WY, Casper, WY, Eugene, OR; **Rod DeHaven**, 9/21/66, Sacramento, CA, Sacramento, CA, Madison, WI; **Pascal Dobert**, 10/27/73,

2000 U.S. Olympic Team Roster

Washington, DC, Washington, DC, Madison, WI; **Jon Drummond**, 9/9/68, Philadelphia, PA, Philadelphia, PA, Culver City, CA; **Philip Dunn**, 6/12/71, Eugene, OR, Chula Vista, CA, Chula Vista, CA; **Kenny Evans**, 6/4/79, Pine Bluff, AR, Pine Bluff, AR, Pine Bluff, AR; **Mark Everett**, 9/2/68, Bagdad, FL, Bagdad, FL, Gainesville, FL; **John Godina**, 5/31/72, Fort Sill, OK, Cheyenne, WY, Northridge, CA; **Adam Goucher**, 2/18/75, Hollywood, FL, Colorado Springs, CO, Boulder, CO; **Breaux Greer**, 10/19/76, Houston, TX, Lafayette, LA, Athens, GA; **Maurice Greene**, 7/24/74, Kansas City, KS, Kansas City, KS, Granada Hills, CA; **Alvin Harrison**, 1/20/74, Orlando, FL, Orlando, FL, Salinas, CA; **Calvin Harrison**, 1/20/74, Orlando, FL, Orlando, FL, Salinas, CA; **Chad Harting**, 2/20/72, St Louis, MO, Jonesboro, AR, Jonesboro, AR; **Brad Hauser**, 3/18/77, Danville, PA, Palo Alto, CA, Palo Alto, CA; **Floyd Heard**, 3/24/66, West Point, MS, Houston, TX, Houston, TX; **Andrew Hermann**, 2/25/71, Newport, OR, Portland, OR, Chula Vista, CA; **Ja'Warren Hooker**, n/a, Chicago, IL, Seattle, WA, Seattle, WA; **Robert Howard**, 11/26/75, Brooklyn, NY, Pawtucket, RI, Fayetteville, AR; **Chris Huffins**, 4/15/70, Brooklyn, NY, Indianapolis, IN, Raleigh, NC; **Nick Hysong**, 12/9/71, Winslow, AZ, Phoenix, AZ, Phoenix, AZ; **Jud Logan**, 7/19/59, Canton, OH, Canton, OH, North Canton, OH; **Kip Janvrin**, 7/8/65, Panora, IA, Panora, IA, Warrensburg, MO; **Gabe Jennings**, 1/25/79, Forks of Salmon, CA, Stanford, CA, Stanford, CA; **Allen Johnson**, 3/1/71, Washington, DC, Washington, DC, Columbia, SC; **Curtis Johnson**, 12/24/73, Palmetto, FL, Palmetto, FL, Inglewood, CA; **Michael Johnson**, 9/13/67, Dallas, TX, Dallas, TX, Waco, TX; **Lawrence Johnson**, 5/7/74, Norfolk, VA, Chesapeake, VA, Knoxville, TN; **Mebrahtom (Meb) Keflezighi**, 5/5/75, Asmara, Eritrea, San Diego, CA, Chula Vista, CA; **Rich Kenah**, 8/4/70, Montclair, NJ, Montclair, NJ, Reston, VA; **Nathan Leeper**, 6/13/77, Greensburg, KS, Protection, KS, Protection, KS; **Brian Lewis**, 12/5/74, Sacramento, CA, Chesapeake, VA, Chesapeake, VA; **Melvin Lister**, 8/29/77, Staten Island, NY, Staten Island, NY, Fayetteville, AR; **Danny McCray**, 3/11/74, Aberdeen, MD, Los Angeles, CA, Los Angeles, CA; **Kevin McMahon**, 5/26/72, San Jose, CA, San Jose, CA, San Jose, CA; **Coby Miller**, 10/19/76, Ackerman, MS, Auburn, AL, Auburn, AL; **Tim Montgomery**, 1/28/75, Gafney, SC, Raleigh, NC, Raleigh, NC; **Adam Nelson**, 7/7/75, Atlanta, GA, Atlanta, GA, San Carlos, CA; **Tom Pappas**, 9/6/75, Roseburg, OR, Azalea, OR, Knoxville, TN; **Antonio Pettigrew**, 11/3/67, Macon, GA, Macon, GA, Raleigh, NC; **Dwight Phillips**, 1/10/77, Decatur, GA, Stone Mountain, GA, Tempe, AZ; **Jason Pyrah**, 4/6/69, Springfield, MO, Springfield, MO, Provo, UT; **Nick Rogers**, 5/2/75, Seattle, WA, Eugene, OR, Eugene, OR; **Tim Seaman**, 5/14/72, North Kingston, RI, Long Island, NY, Chula Vista, CA; **Adam Setliff**, 12/15/69, El Dorado, AZ, Dallas, TX, Valencia, CA; **Michael Stember**, 1/30/78, Fair Oaks, CA, Fair Oaks, CA, Palo Alto, CA; **Savante Stringfellow**, 11/6/78, n/a, n/a, Oxford, MS; **Angelo Taylor**, 12/29/78, Albany, GA, Atlanta, GA, Atlanta, GA; **Eric Thomas**, 12/1/73, Carthage, TX, Garrison, TX, Houston, TX; **Terrence Trammell**, 11/23/78, Atlanta, GA, Decatur, GA, Columbia, SC; **Anthony Washington**, 1/16/66, Glasgow, MT, Rome, NY, Parker, CO; **Bernard Williams III**, 1/19/78, Baltimore, MD, Baltimore, MD, Baltimore, MD; **Bryan Woodward**, 8/3/74, Long Beach, CA, Long Beach, CA, Long Beach, CA; **Jerome Young**, 8/14/76, Hartford, CT, Raleigh, NC, Raleigh, NC
Team Leader: Fred Newhouse, 11/8/48, Honey Grove, TX, Benicia, CA, Benicia, CA
Asst Team Leader: Dixon Farmer, 2/15/41, Minneapolis, MN, Chula Vista, CA, Chula Vista, CA
Head Coach: John Chaplin, 4/9/37, Los Angeles, CA, Palouse, WA, Palouse, WA
Asst Coach: Dick Booth, 7/19/44, Olathe, KS, Fayetteville, AR,

Fayetteville, AR
Asst Coach: Rob Johnson, 2/20/41, Englewood, NJ, Crawfordsville, IN, Crawfordsville, IN
Asst Coach: Johnny Moon, 2/19/38, Prosperity, SC, Somerset, NJ, Somerset, NJ
Asst Coach: Jerry Quiller, 4/28/42, Denver, CO, West Point, NY, West Point, NY
Asst Coach: L Jay Silvester, 8/27/37, Garland, UT, Orem, UT, Orem, UT
Asst Coach: Charles Bubba Thornton, 9/3/47, Fort Worth, TX, Austin, TX, Austin, TX

Athletics Support Personnel:
Team Administrator: Mike Conley, 10/5/62, Chicago, IL, Indianapolis, IN, Indianapolis, IN
Team Liaison: Andrea Johnson, 7/7/66, Clarksville, TN, Indianapolis, IN, Indianapolis, IN
Team Liaison: Bruce Tenen, n/a, n/a, n/a,
Team Support: Keith Henschen, 10/9/43, Fort Wayne, IN, Salt Lake City, UT, Salt Lake City, UT
Team Support: Ralph Vernacchia, 11/6/45, Newark, NJ, Bellingham, WA, Bellingham, WA
Medical Liaison: Richard Strand, 1/19/43, Gainesville, FL, Phoenix, AZ, Phoenix, AZ
Athletic Trainer: Dean Clark, 7/3/52, Portland, OR, West Linn, OR, West Linn, OR
Athletic Trainer: Cheryl Parker, 12/13/61, Charleston, SC, Seattle, WA, Seattle, WA

BADMINTON
Men (1)
Name, Birth date, Birthplace, Hometown, Current Residence
Kevin Han, 11/25/72, Shanghai, China, Colorado Springs, CO, Colorado Springs, CO
Team Leader: Steven Kearney, 3/27/56, Palo Alto, CA, Dunwoody, GA, Dunwoody, GA
National Team Coach: Ardy Wiranata, 2/10/70, Jakarta, Indonesia, Colorado Springs, CO, Colorado Springs, CO

BASEBALL
Men (24)
Name, Birth date, Birthplace, Hometown, Current Residence
Brent Abernathy, 9/23/77, Atlanta, GA, Marietta, GA, Durham, NC; **Kurt Ainsworth**, 9/9/78, Baton Rouge, LA, Kingwood, TX, Shreveport, LA; **Pat Borders**, 5/14/63, Columbus, OH, Lake Wales, FL, Durham, NC; **Sean Burroughs**, 9/12/80, Atlanta, GA, Long Beach, CA, Mobile, AL; **John Cotton**, 10/30/70, Houston, TX, Houston, TX, Colorado Springs, CO; **Travis Dawkins**, 5/12/79, Newberry, SC, Chappells, SC, Chattanooga, TN; **Adam Everett**, 2/6/77, Austell, GA, Kennesaw, GA, New Orleans, LA; **Ryan Franklin**, 3/5/73, Ft Smith, AR, Spiro, OK, Tacoma, WA; **Chris George**, 9/16/79, Houston, TX, Spring, TX, Omaha, NE; **Shane Hearns**, 9/25/75, Toledo, OH, Lambertville, MI, Jacksonville, FL; **Marcus Jensen**, 12/14/72, Oakland, CA, Scottsdale, AZ, Salt Lake City, UT; **Mike Kinkade**, 5/6/73, Livonia, MI, Tigard, OR, Rochester, NY; **Rick Krivda**, 1/19/70, McKeesport, PA, McKeesport, PA, Rochester, NY; **Doug Mientkiewicz**, 6/19/74, Toledo, OH, Miami, FL, Salt Lake City, UT; **Mike Neill**, 4/27/70, Martinsville, VA, Seaford, DE, Tacoma, WA; **Roy Oswalt**, 8/29/77, Kosciusko, MS, Weir, MS, Round Rock, MS; **Jon Rauch**, 9/27/78, Louisville,

Soigneur: Waldemar Stepniowski, 10/28/64, Jelenia, Poland, Littleton, CO, Littleton, CO
Soigneur: Freddy Viaene, 9/9/58, Lendelede, Belgium, Izegem, Belgium, Izegem, Belgium
Soigneur: Aaron Epperson, 7/11/73, Twin Falls, ID, Soldotna, AK, Soldotna, AK

Diving
Women (4)
Name, Birth date, Birthplace, Hometown, Current Residence
Michelle Davison, 10/22/79, Columbia, SC, Columbia, SC, Fort Lauderdale, FL; **Jenny Keim**, 6/17/78, Miami, FL, Miami, FL, Coral Gables, FL; **Sara Reiling**, 9/18/79, Roseville, MN, Roseville, MN, Bloomington, IN; **Laura Wilkinson**, 11/17/77, Houston, TX, Houston, TX, The Wood, TX

Men (3)
Name, Birth date, Birthplace, Hometown, Current Residence
Troy Dumais, 1/21/80, Ventura, CA, Ventura, CA, Ventura, CA; **David Pichler**, 9/3/68, Fort Lauderdale, FL, Fort Lauderdale, FL, Fort Lauderdale, FL; **Mark Ruiz**, 4/9/79, Riopiedra, PR, Orlando, FL, Orlando, FL
Team Leader: Van Austin, 7/14/41, Herrin, IL, Goreville, IL, Goreville, IL
Head Coach: Jay Lerew, 4/8/52, St Louis, MO, Orlando, FL, Orlando, FL
Coach: Randy Ableman, 4/29/59, Cedar Rapids, IA, Miami, FL, Miami, FL
Coach: Ken Armstrong, 10/12/53, Ingersoll, Ontario, Canada, Conroe, TX, Conroe, TX
Coach: Patrick Jeffrey, 6/24/65, Madison, NJ, Morristown, NJ, Tallahasee, FL
Coach: Jeff Huber, 3/28/53, Long Beach, CA, Bloomington, IN, Bloomington, IN
Coach: Tim O'Brien, 7/14/63, Minneapolis, MN, Fort Lauderdale, FL, Fort Lauderdale, FL
Coach: Matt Scoggin, 8/17/63, Saikimken, Japan, Austin, TX, Austin, TX

Equestrian
Dressage (4)
Name, Birth date, Birthplace, Hometown, Current Residence
Sue Blinks, 10/5/57, Washington, DC, Mount Kisco, NY, Wellington, FL; **Robert Dover**, 6/7/56, Chicago, IL, Flemington, NJ, Wellington, FL; **Guenter Seidel**, 9/23/60, Obeisdorf, Germany, Del Mar, CA, Del Mar, CA; **Christine Traurig**, 3/13/57, Nienburg, Germany, Carlsbad, CA, Carlsbad, CA; **Dressage Team Leader: Maureen Pethick**, 9/5/64, Bronx, NY, Califon, NJ, Califon, NJ
Dressage Chef d'Equipe: Jessica Ransenhousen, 10/14/38, London, England, Unionville, PA, Unionville, PA
Groom for Sue Blinks: Christina Baxter, 6/29/74, Huntingdon, PA, Huntingdon, PA, Huntingdon, PA
Groom for Robert Dover: Jessica Van Langen, 3/8/81, n/a, Wellington, FL, Wellington, FL
Groom for Guenter Seidel: Bettina Loy, 3/11/63, Amberg, Germany, Poway, CA, Poway, CA
Groom for Christine Traurig: Joseph Moss, 8/4/58, Oltey, West Yorkshire, UK, Santa Monica, CA, Santa Monica, CA

Jumping (4)

Nona Garson, 9/30/58, Westfield, NJ, Lebanon, NJ, Lebanon, NJ; **Margie Goldstein-Engle**, 3/31/58, Miami, FL, Wellington, FL, Wellington, FL; **Lauren Hough**, 4/11/77, Wellington, FL, Wellington, FL, Ocala, FL; **Laura Kraut**, 11/14/65, Camden, SC, Oconomowoc, WI, Oconomowoc, WI
Jumping Team Leader: Sally Ike, 9/6/44, Long Branch, NJ, Oldwick, NJ, Oldwick, NJ
Jumping Chef d'Equipe: Frank Chapot, 2/24/32, Camden, NJ, Neshanic Station, NJ, Neshanic Station, NJ
Groom for Nona Garson: Antoine Renault, 12/27/71, Issy Les Moulin, France, Lebanon, NJ, Lebanon, NJ
Groom for Goldstein-Engle: Craig Pollard, 10/8/70, Leeds, Yorkshire, England, Lakeworth, FL, Lakeworth, FL
Groom for Lauren Hough: Christy Merkely, 6/29/65, Ottawa, Ont, Canada, Oldwick, NJ, Oldwick, NJ
Groom for Laura Kraut: Oliver O'Toole, n/a, Tipperary, Ireland, Oconomowoc, WI, Oconomowoc, WI

THREE-DAY EVENT (7)
Julie Black, 9/26/70, Montgomery, AL, Newnan, GA, Newnan, GA; **Rebecca (Becky) Douglas**, 4/24/69, n/a, Lansing, KS, Lansing, KS; **Nina Fout**, 6/23/59, Washington, DC, Middleburg, VA, Middleburg, VA; **Karen O'Connor**, 2/17/58, Concord, MA, The Plains, VA, The Plains, VA; **Robert Costello**, 7/26/65, Beverly, MA, Southern Pines, NC, Southern Pines, NC; **David O'Connor**, 1/18/62, Washington, DC, The Plains, VA, The Plains, VA; **Linden Wiesman**, 1/23/75, Columbia, TN, Bluemont, VA, Bluemont, VA
Three-Day Team Leader: Jim Wolf, 8/1/63, Nurnberg, Germany, Gladstone, NJ, Gladstone, NJ
Three-Day Chef d'Equipe: Cpt. Mark Phillips, 9/22/48, Tetburg, Glos UK, Tetburg, Glos UK, Tetburg, Glos UK
Groom for Julie Black: Melissa Silverman
Groom for Robert Costello: Katherine McCall
Groom for Nina Fout: Linda Vegher
Groom for Rebecca Douglas: Vicki Baker
Groom for Linden Wiesman: Emile Hart
Groom for David O'Connor: Colleen Hayduk
Groom for David O'Connor: Joanne Wilson
Groom for Karen O'Connor: Nicole Beauchane

Equestrian Support Personnel:
Asst Chef de Equipe: George Morris, 2/16/38, New York, NY, Pittstown, NJ, Pittstown, NJ
Dressage Veterinarian: Midge Leitch, 2/27/46, Philadelphia, PA, Cochranville, PA, Cochranville, PA
Jumping Veterinarian: Rick Mitchell, 9/20/49, Greensboro, NC, Easton, CT, Easton, CT
Three-Day Veterinarian: Brendan Furlong, 5/16/53, Wexford, Ireland, Pittstown, NJ, Pittstown, NJ
Three-Day Veterinarian: Patrick McMahon, 12/8/47, Clonmel, Ireland, Plaistow Billingshurst, UK, Plaistow Billingshurst, UK
Dressage/Jumping Stable Manager: Francisco Alvarez, 9/17/47, Middleburg, VA, Middleburg, VA
Stable Manager: Eric Stauffer, 11/8/71, Scranton, PA, Middlesburg, VA, Middlesburg, VA
Farrier: Steve Teichman, 9/18/58, Villanova, PA, East Fallowfeil, PA, East Fallowfeil, PA
Medical Liaison: Craig Farrell, n/a, n/a, n/a, n/a

Fencing
Women (4)

2000 U.S. Olympic Team Roster

Name, Birth date, Birthplace, Hometown, Current Residence
Ann Marsh, 6/30/71, Royal Oak, MI, Royal Oak, MI, Rochester, NY; **Arlene Stevens**, 2/20/81, Rochester, NY, Fresh Meadow, NY, Fresh Meadow, NY; **Felicia Zimmermann**, 8/16/75, Rochester, NY, Rush, NY, Palo Alto, CA; **Iris Zimmermann**, 1/6/81, Rochester, NY, Rush, NY, Palo Alto, CA

Men (4)
Name, Birth date, Birthplace, Hometown, Current Residence
Clifford Bayer, 6/14/77, New York, NY, New York, NY, New York, NY; **Tamir Bloom**, 12/24/71, New York, NY, Millburn, NJ, New York, NY; **Keeth Smart**, 7/29/78, Brooklyn, NY, Brooklyn, NY, Brooklyn, NY; **Akhnaten Spencer-El**, 4/13/79, Baltimore, MD, Harlem, NY, Harlem, NY
Team Leader: Robert Largman, 11/18/61, Morristown, NJ, Morristown, NJ, Morristown, NJ
Men's Coach: Anthony (Buckie) Leach, 9/22/58, Elmira, NY, Rochester, NY, Rochester, NY
Women's Coach: Yefim Litvan, 2/4/40, Khankov, Ukraine, Milburn, NJ, Milburn, NJ

Fencing Support Personnel:
Team Captain: Carl Borack, 7/12/47, Staten Island, NY, Beverly Hills, CA, Beverly Hills, CA
Team Administrator: Carla Mae Richards, 4/7/36, New York, NY, Peyton, CO, Peyton, CO
Armorer: Matthew Porter, 2/2/57, Groton, CT, Pacifica, CA, Pacifica, CA
Personal Coach: Aladar Kogler, 12/22/33, Slovakia, New York, NY, New York, NY
Personal Coach: Yuri Gelman, 10/13/55, Kiev, Ukraine, Brooklyn, NY, Brooklyn, NY

GYMNASTICS
ARTISTIC
Women (6)
Amy Chow, 5/15/78, San Jose, CA, San Jose , CA, San Jose, CA; **Jamie Dantzscher**, 5/2/82, Canoga Park, CA, Palmdale , CA, San Dimas, CA; **Dominique Dawes**, 11/20/76, Silver Spring, MD, Silver Spring, MD, Silver Spring, MD; **Kristen Maloney**, 3/10/81, Hackerstown, NJ, Pen Argyl, PA, Pen Argyl, PA; **Elise Ray**, 2/6/82, Tallahassee, FL, Columbia , MD, Columbia, MD; **Tasha Schwikert**, 11/21/85, Las Vegas, NV, Las Vegas, NV, Las Vegas, NV
Team Leader: Kathy Kelly, 11/6/47, St Louis, MO, Indianapolis, IN, Indianapolis, IN
Head Coach: Kelli Hill
Assistant Coach: Steve Rybacki
National Team Coordinator: Bela Karolyi
Personal Coach: Donna Strauss
Personal Coach: Mark Young

Men (6)
Morgan Hamm, 9/24/82, Ashland, WI, Waukesha , WI, Waukesha, WI; **Paul Hamm**, 9/24/82, Washburn, WI, Waukesha , WI, Waukesha, WI; **Stephen McCain**, 1/9/74, Houston, TX, Houston , TX, Colorado Springs, CO; **John Roethlisberger**, 6/21/70, Fort Atkinson, WI, Falcon Heights , MN, Falcon Heights, MN; **Sean Townsend**, 1/20/79, Temple, TX, Dallas , TX, Houston, TX; **Blaine Wilson**, 8/3/74, Columbus, OH, Columbus , OH, Colorado Springs, CO
Team Leader: Ron Galimore, 3/7/59, Tallahassee, FL, Indianapolis, IN, Indianapolis, IN
Head Coach: Peter Kormann, 6/21/55, Boston, MA, Westerville, OH, Westerville, OH
Assistant Coach: Yoichi Tomita
Assistant Coach: Barry Weiner

Gymnastics Support Personnel:
Personal Coach: Ronald Brant
Personal Coach: William Maloney
Personal Coach: Vitaly Marinitch
Personal Coach: Kevin Mazeika
Personal Coach: Thomas Glielmi

TRAMPOLINE
Women (1)
Name, Birth date, Birthplace, Hometown, Current Residence
Jennifer Parilla, 1/9/81, Newport Beach, CA, Lake Forest, CA, Lake Forest, CA
Trampoline Team Leader: Ann Sims, 10/5/48, Levelland, TX, Brownfield, TX, Brownfield, TX
Coach: Robert Null, 4/6/50, Riverside, CA, Mission Viejo, CA, Mission Viejo, CA

JUDO
Women (7)
Name, Birth date, Birthplace, Hometown, Current Residence
Sandra Bacher, 5/28/68, Bay Shore, NY, San Jose, CA, San Jose, CA; **Lauren Meece**, 2/6/83, Hollywood, CA, Pembroke Pines, FL, Pembroke Pines, FL; **Colleen Rosensteel**, 3/13/67, Greensburg, PA, Buffalo Grove, IL, Buffalo Grove, IL; **Celita Schutz**, 2/17/68, Houston, TX, Hillsdale, NJ, Westwood, NJ; **Amy Tong**, 10/18/77, Honolulu, HI, San Jose, CA, San Jose, CA; **Bernice (Ellen) Wilson**, 1/8/76, Salinas, CA, Salinas, CA, Colorado Springs, CO; **Hillary Wolf**, 2/7/77, Chicago, IL, Chicago, IL, Colorado Springs, CO

Men (7)
Name, Birth date, Birthplace, Hometown, Current Residence
Martin Boonzaayer, 11/1/72, Kalamazoo, MI, Palatine, IL, Palatine, IL; **Brandon Greczkowski**, 7/18/77, Putnam, CT, Colorado Springs, CO, Colorado Springs, CO; **Ato Hand**, 6/30/75, Tallahassee, FL, Tallahassee, FL, Colorado Springs, CO; **Jason Morris**, 2/3/67, Scotia, NY, Scotia, NY, Scotia, NY; **Brian Olson**, 3/6/73, Tallahassee, FL, Woodville, FL, Colorado Springs, CO; **Alex Ottiano**, 2/4/76, Providence, RI, Oneco, CT, Oneco, CT; **James Pedro**, 10/30/70, Danvers, MA, Lawrence, MA, Lawrence, MA
Team Leader: James Colgan, 3/17/31, Chicago, IL, Elk Grove Village, IL, Elk Grove Village, IL
Team Leader: Lou Moyerman, 3/6/52, Philadelphia, PA, Philadelphia, PA, Philadelphia, PA
Men's Coach: Steve Cohen, 8/29/55, Chicago, IL, Wheeling, IL, Wheeling, IL
Women's Coach: Edward Liddie, 7/24/59, Delones, France, Colorado Springs, CO, Colorado Springs, CO

Judo Support Personnel:
Assistant Coach: Irwin Cohen, 1/21/52, Chicago, IL, Buffalo Grove, IL, Buffalo Grove, IL
Assistant Coach: Evelio Garcia, 12/11/50, Havana, Cuba, Miami, FL, Miami, FL

2000 U.S. Olympic Team Roster

MODERN PENTATHLON

Women (2)

Name, Birth date, Birthplace, Hometown, Current Residence

Emily de Riel, 11/12/74, Boston, MA, Havertown, PA, San Antonio, TX; **Mary Beth Larsen Iagorshvili**, 7/28/74, Mukwonago, WI, Mukwonago, WI, San Antonio, TX

Men (2)

Name, Birth date, Birthplace, Hometown, Current Residence

Velizar Iliev, 3/9/66, Vratza, Bulgaria, Vratza, Bulgaria, San Antonio, TX; **Chad Senior**, 12/27/74, Ft Myers, FL, Ft Myers, FL, Colorado Springs, CO

Team Leader: Jim Gregory, 8/3/70, Manassas, VA, Colorado Springs, CO, Colorado Springs, CO

Women's Coach: Victor Svatenko, 7/1/43, Poltava, Ukraine, San Antonio, TX, San Antonio, TX

Men's Coach: Janusz Peciak, 2/9/49, Warsaw, Poland, Denver, CO, Denver, CO

Modern Pentathlon Support Personnel:

Riding Coach: Shane Brasher, 2/1/52, Espanola, NM, San Antonio, TX, San Antonio, TX

Shooting Coach: Vaho Iagorashvili, 4/5/64, Tibilisi, Georgia, San Antonio, TX, San Antonio, TX

ROWING

Women (20)

Name, Birth date, Birthplace, Hometown, Current Residence

Christine Smith Collins, 9/9/69, Mt. Kisco, NY, Darien, CT, Worcester, MA; **Ruth Davidon**, 3/20/64, New York, NY, Haverford, PA, San Francisco, CA; **Jennifer Dore-Terhaar**, 12/19/71, Montclair, NJ, Kearney, NJ, Augusta, GA; **Torrey Folk**, 12/10/73, Ann Arbor, MI, Columbia, MO, Chula Vista, CA; **Amy Fuller**, 5/30/68, Inglewood, CA, Thousand Oaks, CA, Chula Vista, CA; **Sarah Garner**, 5/21/71, Kaiserslautern, Germany, Madison, WI, Princeton, NJ; **Hilary Gehman**, 8/15/71, Shirley, MA, Wolfeboro, NH, Augusta, GA; **Sarah Jones**, 8/26/73, Olympia, WA, Starwood, WA, Camino Island, WA; **Laurel Korholz**, 6/10/70, New York City, NY, Rancho Santa Fe, CA, Augusta, GA; **Karen Kraft**, 5/3/69, San Mateo, CA, San Mateo, CA, Princeton; **Katie Maloney**, 3/22/74, Cleveland, OH, Seattle, WA, Chula Vista, CA; **Amy Martin**, 11/4/74, Hood River, OR, Kent, OR, Chula Vista, CA; **Betsy McCagg**, 4/29/67, Seattle, WA, Kirkland, WA, Kirkland, WA; **Monica Tranel Michini**, 5/4/66, Big Horn, WY, Missoula, MT, Missoula, MT; **Linda Miller**, 10/16/72, Washington, DC, Alexandria, VA, Chula Vista, CA; **Lianne Nelson**, 6/15/72, Houston, TX, Seattle, WA, Chula Vista, CA; **Missy Ryan**, 7/17/72, Bloomington, IN, Bloomington, IN, Princeton, NJ; **Kelly Salchow**, 10/5/73, Cincinnati, OH, Cincinnati, OH, Augusta, GA; **Rajanya Shah**, 2/16/74, Albany, NY, North Greenbush, NY, Chula Vista, CA; **Carol Skricki**, 7/27/62, Norwood, MA, Norwood, MA, Augusta, GA

Men (28)

Name, Birth date, Birthplace, Hometown, Current Residence

Christian Ahrens, 7/24/76, Iowa City, IA, Milwaukee, WI, Princeton, NJ; **Tom Auth**, 9/9/68, Orange, NJ, Maplewood, NJ, New York, NY; **Sebastian Bea**, 4/10/77, San Francisco, CA, San Francisco, CA, San Francisco, CA; **Peter Cipollone**, 2/5/71, Marietta, OH, Ardmore, PA, Princeton, NJ; **Atwood (Porter) Collins**, 6/27/75, New York, NY, Darien, CT, Princeton, NJ; **Mike**

Ferry, 4/13/74, Princeton, NJ, Princeton, NJ, Augusta, GA; **Conal Groom**, 5/16/73, New Haven, CT, Northford, CT, Boston, MA; **Michael (Sean) Hall**, 8/20/67, Williamsburg, VA, Arlington, VA, Chula Vista, CA; **Robert (Bob) Kaehler**, 4/5/64, , Huntington, NY, Holland, PA; **Jeffery Klepacki**, 12/17/68, Kearny, NJ, Kearny, NJ, Princeton, NJ; **James Koven**, 4/18/73, Morristown, NJ, Green Village, NJ, Kingston, NJ; **Ian McGowan**, 5/23/79, Seattle, WA, Snohomish, WA, Augusta, GA; **Garrett Miller**, 6/7/77, Philadelphia, PA, Philadelphia, PA, Erdenheim, PA; **Wolfgang Moser**, 12/3/74, Laconia, NH, Moultonboro, NH, Princeton, NJ; **Eric Mueller**, 11/6/70, Kansas City, MO, Cedarburg, WI, Princeton, NJ; **Ted Murphy**, 10/30/71, West Newton, MA, West Newton, MA, Princeton, NJ; **Henry Nuzum**, 3/4/77, Chapel Hill, NC, Chapel Hill, NC, Chapel Hill, NC; **Nicholas Peterson**, 2/23/73, Alexandria, VA, Alexandria, VA, Augusta, GA; **Gregory (Greg) Ruckman**, 12/30/73, Cincinnati, OH, Cincinnati, OH, Camano Island, WA; **Marc Schneider**, 4/28/73, Lubbock, TX, Everett, WA, Princeton, NJ; **David (Dave) Simon**, 12/2/79, , West Bloomfield, MI, West Bloomfield, MI; **Donald (Don) Smith**, 4/7/68, North Tonawanda, NY, Buffalo, NY, Philadelphia, PA; **Paul Teti**, 2/5/77, Drexel, PA, Upper Darby, PA, Upper Darby, PA; **Robert (Steve) Tucker**, 3/3/69, Indianapolis, IN, Mooresville, IN, Boston, MA; **Bryan Volpenhein**, 8/18/76, Cincinnati, OH, Cincinnati, OH, Princeton, NJ; **Tom Welsh**, 5/6/77, Philadelphia, PA, Huntingdon Valley, PA, Princeton, NJ; **Jacob (Jake) Wetzel**, 12/26/76, Saskatoon, Canada, Saskatoon, Canada, Berkley, CA; **Michael Wherley**, 3/15/72, Waconia, MN, Sun Prairie, WI, Yardley, PA

Team Leader: Mark Sniderman, 8/21/70, Toronto, Ont, Canada, Indianapolis, IN, Indianapolis, IN

Asst Team Leader: Willie Black, 8/19/60, Seattle, WA, Indianapolis, IN, Indianapolis, IN

Boat Coaches:

Hartmut Buschbacher - Women's Eight; Jim Dietz - Women's Ltwt Double Sculls; Igor Grinko - Men's Quad; Angie Herron - Women's Single Sculls; Curtis Jordan - Men's Ltwt Four; Ted Nash - Men's Double; John Pescatore - Men's Pair; Mike Porterfield - Women's Pair; Mike Teti - Men's Eight

Rowing Support Personnel:

Team Administrator: Mary Kramer, 7/4/66, Wadsworth, OH, Indianapolis, IN, Indianapolis, IN

Boat Handler: Brad Woodrick, n/a, n/a, n/a, n/a

Boat Coaches:

Charlie Butt - Men's Ltwt Double Sculls; Dick Garrard - Men's Singles Sculls; David Gleeson - Women's Double Sculls; Tom Terhaar - Women's Quad; Gavin White - Men's Four

SAILING

Women (4)

Name, Birth date, Birthplace, Hometown, Current Residence

Courtenay Becker-Dey, 4/27/65, Rye, NY, Rye, NY, The Dalles, OR; **Lanee Butler**, 6/3/70, Manhasset, NY, Aliso Viejo, CA, Aliso Viejo, CA; **Sarah (Pease) Glaser**, 11/18/61, Springfield, IL, Long Beach, CA, Long Beach, CA; **Jennifer (JJ) Isler**, 12/1/63, La Jolla, CA, La Jolla, CA, La Jolla, CA

Men (14)

Name, Birth date, Birthplace, Hometown, Current Residence

Paul Foerster, 11/19/63, Alice, TX, Garland, TX, Garland, TX; **Michael Gebhardt**, 11/25/65, Columbus, OH, Fort Pierce, FL, Fort

Pierce, FL; **Craig Healy**, 9/9/57, San Pablo, CA, Port Richmond, CA, Tiburon, CA; **Hartwell Jordan**, 12/8/61, Oakland, CA, Piedmont, CA, Discovery Bay, CA; **Magnus Liljedahl**, 3/6/54, Miami, FL, Miami, FL, Miami, FL; **John Lovell**, 3/31/68, Baton Rouge, LA, New Orleans, LA, New Orleans, LA; **Jeff Madrigali**, 5/8/56, Walnut Creek, CA, Ross, CA, Novato, CA; **Charlie McKee**, 3/14/62, Seattle, WA, Seattle, WA, Seattle, WA; **Jonathan McKee**, 12/19/59, Seattle, WA, Seattle, WA, Seattle, WA; **Robert Merrick**, 1/18/71, New York, NY, Portsmouth, RI, Portsmouth, RI; **John Myrdal**, 6/3/71, Kailua, HI, Kailua, HI, Kailua, HI; **Charlie Ogletree**, 3/31/68, Greenville, NC, Columbia, NC, Long Beach, CA; **Mark Reynolds**, 3/31/56, San Diego, CA, San Diego, CA, San Diego, CA; **Russell Silverstri**, 10/12/61, San Francisco, CA, San Francisco, CA, San Francisco, CA

Team Leader: Hal Haenel, 10/18/58, St Louis, MO, Los Angeles, CA, Los Angeles, CA

Boatwright: Carl Eichenlaub, 6/7/30, San Diego, CA, San Diego, CA, San Diego, CA

Head Coach: Gary Bodie, 12/1/55, Norfolk, VA, Hampton, VA, Hampton, VA

Sailing Support Personnel:

Team Administrator: Jonathan Harley, 9/5/44, Providence, RI, Middletown, RI, Middletown, RI

Finn Coach: James Worthington, 4/7/60, Santa Monica, CA, Orinda, CA, Orinda, CA

Mistral Coach: Pierce Jeangirard, 10/13/54, Paris, France, Bishop, CA, Bishop, CA

Soling Coach: Russell Coutts, n/a, n/a, New Zealand, New Zealand

Star Coach: Ed Adams, 9/12/56, Providence, RI, Middletown, RI, Middletown, RI

Tornado Coach: Jay Glaser, 7/11/53, Santa Monica, CA, Long Beach, CA, Long Beach, CA

470 Coach: Skip White, n/a, n/a, n/a, n/a

49er Coach: Luther Carpenter, 4/20/62, Atlanta, GA, New Orleans, LA, New Orleans, LA

Shooting
Women (11)
Name, Birth date, Birthplace, Hometown, Current Residence
Janine Bowman, 3/15/73, Norwood, MA, Woonsocket, RI, Dallas, TX; **Christina Cassidy**, 1/12/82, Oceanside, CA, Escondido, CA, Escondido, CA; **Jayme Dickman**, 7/30/77, South Bend, IN, South Bend, IN, Sharpsburg, GA; **Jean Foster**, 10/3/72, Columbus, GA, Bozeman, MT, Colorado Springs, CO; **Cindy Gentry**, 10/14/54, Fort Worth, TX, Stone Mountain, GA, Atlanta, GA; **Nancy Johnson**, 1/14/74, Hinsdale, IL, Downers Grove, IL, Phenix City, AL; **Thrine Kane**, 5/24/81, Rockville Centre, NY, Merrick, NY, Merrick, NY; **Melissa Mulloy**, 3/16/78, Danvers, MA, Middleton MA, Fairbanks, AK; **Kimberly (Kim) Rhode**, 7/16/79, Whittier, CA, El Monte, CA, El Monte, CA; **Cindy Shenberger**, 6/12/69, Vallejo, CA, Corona, CA, Hope Mills, NC; **Rebecca (Beki) Snyder**, 6/15/76, Didsbury, Alb, Canada, Grand Junction, CO, Colorado Springs, CO

Men (17)
Name, Birth date, Birthplace, Hometown, Current Residence
Michael Anti, 2/8/64, Orange, CA, Winterville, NC, Fort Benning, GA; **Lance Bade**, 2/6/71, Vancouver, WA, Vancouver, WA, Colorado Springs, CO; **Bill Demarest**, 12/20/64, Worcester, MA, Orange County, CA, Lake Forest, CA; **Lance Dement**, 9/20/68, Honolulu, HI, Runge, TX, Seale, AL; **Mike Douglass**, 5/1/76, Portsmouth, VA,

Beach Park, IL, Colorado Springs, CO; **Glenn Dubis**, 2/5/59, Lincoln, NE, Bethel Park, PA, Columbus, GA; **Glenn Eller**, 1/6/82, Houston, TX, Katy, TX, Katy, TX; **James (Todd) Graves**, 3/27/63, Rustin, LA, laurel, MS, Cusseta, GA; **Ken Johnson**, 11/24/68, Quincy, MA, Marshfield, MA, Phenix City, AL; **Bill Keever**, 3/14/76, Rutherfordton, NC, Rutherfordton, NC, Phenix City, AL; **Josh Lakatos**, 3/24/73, Pasadena, CA, Pasadena, CA, Pasadena, CA; **John McNally**, 1/20/56, Naha Okinawa, Japan, Heath, TX, Heath, TX; **Jason Parker**, 6/27/74, Omaha, NE, Omaha, NE, Columbus, GA; **Adam Saathoff**, 5/25/75, Tucson, AZ, Hereford, AZ, Colorado Springs, CO; **Mike Schmidt Jr.**, 4/15/58, Decatur, IL, Eagan, MN, Eagan, MN; **Daryl Szarenski**, 3/14/68, Saginaw, MI, Saginaw, MI, Seale, AL; **Tom Tamas**, 6/11/65, Columbus, GA, Columbus, GA, Columbus, GA; **Team Leader: Bob Mitchell**, 5/6/47, Fremont, OH, Littleton, CO, Littleton, CO; **Pistol Coach: Erich Buljung**, 3/21/44, Yugoslavia, Colorado Springs, CO, Colorado Springs, CO; **Rifle Coach: Dan Durben**, 5/2/59, St Paul, MN, Belle Fourche, SD, Belle Fourche, SD; **Running Target Coach: Sergey Luzov**, 5/26/59, Potsdam, Germany, Colorado Springs, CO, Colorado Springs, CO; **Clay Target Coach: Lloyd Woodhouse**, 5/14/35, Norfolk, VA, Colorado Springs, CO, Colorado Springs, CO; **Armorer: Scott Pilkington**, 2/27/64, Rantoul, IL, Monteague, TN, Monteague, TN

Soccer
Women (18)
Name, Birth date, Birthplace, Hometown, Current Residence
Brandi Chastain, 7/21/68, San Jose, CA, San Jose, CA, San Jose, CA; **Lorrie Fair**, 8/5/78, Los Altos, CA, Los Altos, CA, Chapel Hill, NC; **Joy Fawcett**, 2/8/68, Inglewood, CA, Huntington Beach, CA, Los Angeles, CA; **Julie Foudy**, 1/23/71, San Diego, CA, Mission Viejo, CA, Mission Viejo, CA; **Michelle French**, 1/27/77, n/a, n/a, n/a; **Mia Hamm**, 3/17/72, Selma, AL, Chapel Hill, NC, Chapel Hill, NC; **Kristine Lilly**, 7/22/71, New York, NY, Wilton, CT, Wilton, CT; **Shannon MacMillan**, 10/7/74, Syosset, NY, Escondido, CA, Portland, OR; **Tiffeny Milbrett**, 10/23/72, Portland, OR, Portland, OR, Portland, OR; **Siri Mullinix**, 5/22/78, Denver, CO, Greensboro, NC, Greensboro, NC; **Carla Overbeck**, 5/9/68, Pasadena, CA, Dallas, TX, Duram, NC; **Cindy Parlow**, 5/8/78, Memphis, TN, Memphis, TN, Memphis, TN; **Christie Pearce**, 6/24/75, Broward County, FL, Point Pleasant, NJ, n/a; **Briana Scurry**, 9/7/71, Minneapolis, MN, Dayton, MN, Dayton, MN; **Nikki Serlenga**, 6/20/78, San Diego, CA, San Diego, CA, San Diego, CA; **Danielle Slaton**, 6/1/80, n/a, San Jose, CA, n/a; **Kate Sobrero**, 8/23/76, Pontiac, MI, Bloomfield Hills, MI, Bloomfield Hills, MI; **Sara Whalen**, 4/28/76, Natick, MA, Greenlawn, NY, Stoors, CT

Team Leader: Nils Krumins, 3/8/69, Cleveland, OH, Chicago, IL, Chicago, IL

Head Coach: April Heinrichs, 2/27/64, Denver, CO, Charlottesville, VA, Charlottesville, VA

Asst Coach: John Ellis, 4/13/39, Dartford, England, Manassas, VA, Manassas, VA

Asst Coach: Colleen Hacker, 11/24/56, Lancaster, PA, Tacoma, WA, Tacoma, WA

Soccer Support Personnel:

Goalkeeper Coach: Dave Vanole, 2/6/63, Redondo Beach, CA, Manhattan Beach, CA, Manhattan Beach, CA

Equipment Manager: Dainis Kalnins, 11/26/68, Des Moines, IA, Chicago, IL, Chicago, IL

Men (18)

Name, Birth date, Birthplace, Hometown, Current Residence
Jeff Agoos, 5/2/68, Geneva, Switzerland, Dallas, TX, Washington, DC; **Chris Albright**, 1/14/79, Philadelphia, PA, Philadelphia, PA, Washington, DC; **Danny Califf**, 3/17/80, Montclair, CA, Orange, CA, Los Angeles, CA; **Conor Casey**, 7/25/81, Dover, NH, Denver, CO, Portland, OR; **Ramiro Corrales**, 3/12/77, Los Angeles, CA, Salinas, CA; **Joey DiGiamarino**, 4/6/77, n/a, Corona, CA, Denver, CO; **Landon Donovan**, 3/4/82, Redlands, CA, Redlands, CA, Redlands, CA; **Brian Dunseth**, 3/2/77, Upland, CA, Upland, CA, Boston, MA; **Brad Friedel**, 5/18/71, Lakewood, OH, Bay Village, OH, Bay Village, OH; **Frankie Hejduk**, 8/5/74, La Mesa, CA, Cardiff, CA, Germany; **Tim Howard**, 3/6/79, North Brunswick, NJ, North Brunswick, NJ, n/a; **Chad McCarty**, 10/5/77, Fresno, CA, Clovis, CA, Tampa Bay, FL; **John O'Brien**, 8/29/77, n/a, Playa del Rey, CA, The Netherlands; **Benjamin Olsen**, 5/3/77, Harrisburg, PA, Middletown, PA, Washington, DC; **Peter Vagenas**, 2/6/78, Pasadena, CA, Cerritos, CA, Los Angeles, CA; **Sasha Victorine**, 2/2/78, n/a, Carmichael, CA, Carmichael, CA; **Evan Whitfield**, 6/23/77, n/a, Phoenix, AZ, Chicago, IL; **Josh Wolff**, 2/15/77, Stone Mountain, GA, Stone Mountain, GA, Chicago, IL
Team Leader: Craig Blazer, 11/18/68, Cincinnati, OH, Chicago, IL, Chicago, IL
Head Coach: Clive Charles, 10/3/51, London, England, Portland, OR, Portland, OR
Asst Coach: John Ellinger, 10/4/51, Laurel, MD, Ellicott City, MD, Ellicott City, MD
Goalkeeper Coach: Peter Mellor, 11/20/47, Prestbury, Cheshire, UK, Palm Harbor, FL, Palm Harbor, FL

Soccer Support Personnel:
Equipment Manager: Aaron Barrett, 5/7/75, New Bedford, MA, Chicago, IL, Chicago, IL
Scout Coach: Jay Hoffman, 1/15/51, Womelsdorf, PA, Chagrin Falls, OH, Chagrin Falls, OH

SOFTBALL
Women (15)
Name, Birth date, Birthplace, Hometown, Current Residence
Christie Ambrosi, 12/21/76, Kansas City, MO, Overland Park, KS, Los Angeles, CA; **Laura Berg**, 1/6/75, Whittier, CA, Santa Fe Springs, CA, Fresno, CA; **Jennifer Brundage**, 6/27/73, Orange, CA, Irvine, CA, Ann Arbor, MI; **Crystl Bustos**, 9/8/77, Westminster, CA, Canyon Country, CA, Canyon Country, CA; **Shelia Douty**, 2/26/62, Encino, CA, Diamond Bar, CA, Diamond Bar, CA; **Lisa Fernandez**, 2/22/71, Lakewood, CA, Long Beach, CA, Long Beach, CA; **Lori Harrigan**, 9/5/70, Anaheim, CA, Las Vegas, NV, Las Vegas, NV; **Danielle Henderson**, 1/29/77, Comack, NY, Commack, NY, Amherst, MA; **Jennifer McFalls**, 11/10/71, Arlington, TX, Grand Prairie, TX, Nashville, TN; **Stacey Nuveman**, 4/26/78, Verdugo Hills, CA, LaVerne, CA, Los Angeles, CA; **Leah O'Brien-Amico**, 9/9/74, Garden Grove, CA, Chino, CA, Chino Hills, CA; **Dot Richardson**, 9/22/61, Orlando, CA, Orlando, FL, Los Angeles, CA; **Michele Smith**, 6/21/67, Plainfield, NJ, Califon, NJ, Orlando, FL; **Michelle Venturella**, 5/11/73, Gary, IN, South Holland, IL, Indianapolis, IN; **Christa Williams**, 2/8/78, Houston, TX, Houston, TX, Houston, TX
Team Leader: Ralph Weekly, 11/27/42, Los Angeles, CA, Oklahoma City, OK, Oklahoma City, OK
Head Coach: Ralph Raymond, 4/27/24, Worcester, MA, Worcester, MA, Worcester, MA
Asst Coach: Margo Jonker, 1/20/54, Holland, MI, Mt Pleasant, MI, Mt Pleasant, MI

Asst Coach: Shirley Topley, 4/14/34, Hondo, Alberta, Canada, Anaheim, CA, Anaheim, CA

SWIMMING
Women (24)
Name, Birth date, Birthplace, Hometown, Current Residence
Amanda Adkins, 12/5/76, Peoria, IL, Gahanna, OH, Gahanna, OH; **Samantha Arsenault**, 10/11/81, Peabody, MA, Peabody, MA, n/a; **Amanda Beard**, 10/29/81, Newport Beach, CA, Irvine, CA, Irvine, CA; **Barbara (BJ) Bedford**, 11/9/72, Hanover, NH, Hanover, NH, Colorado Springs, CO; **Lindsay Benko**, 11/29/76, Elkhart, IN, Los Angeles, CA, Los Angeles, CA; **Brooke Bennett**, 5/6/80, Tampa, FL, Tampa, FL, Plant City, FL; **Kim Black**, 4/30/78, Liverpool, NY, Athens, GA, n/a; **Madeline (Maddy) Crippen**, 7/10/80, Conshohocken, PA, Philadelphia, PA, Philadelphia, PA; **Misty Hyman**, 3/23/79, Mesa, AZ, Mesa, AZ, Phoenix, AZ; **Kristy Kowal**, 10/9/78, Reading, PA, Reading, PA, Athens, GA; **Diana Munz**, 6/19/82, Moreland Hills, OH, Chagrin Falls, OH, Chagrin Falls, OH; **Rada Owen**, 10/12/78, Richmond, VA, Chesterfield, VA, Auburn, AL; **Erin Phenix**, 3/1/81, n/a, Cincinnati, OH, Austin, TX; **Megan Quann**, 1/15/84, Tacoma, WA, Puyallup, WA, Puyallup, WA; **Gabrielle Rose**, 11/1/77, n/a, Memphis, TN, Rancho Santa Margarita, CA; **Kaitlin Sandeno**, 3/13/83, n/a, Lake Forest, CA, Lake Forest, CA; **Courtney Shealy**, 12/12/77, Columbia, SC, Columbia, SC, Athens, GA; **Stacianna Stitts**, 9/12/81, Columbus, OH, Carlsbad, CA, Carlsbad, CA; **Julia Stowers**, 3/18/82, Knoxville, TN, Knoxville, TN, Knoxville, TN; **Ashley Tappin**, 12/18/74, Marietta, GA, New Orleans, LA, Colorado Springs, CO; **Christina Teuscher**, 3/12/78, Bronx, NY, New Rochelle, NY, New Rochelle; **Jenny Thompson**, 2/26/73, Danvers, MA, Danvers, MA, Menlo Park, CA; **Dara Torres**, 4/15/67, Beverly Hills, CA, Beverly Hills, CA, Palo Alto, CA; **Amy Van Dyken**, 2/15/73, Denver, CO, Denver, CO, Lone Tree, CO

Men (24)
Name, Birth date, Birthplace, Hometown, Current Residence
Pat Calhoun, 6/16/81, n/a, Seymour, IN, Seymour, IN; **Chad Carvin**, 4/13/74, Laguna Hills, CA, Laguna Hills, CA, Laguna Hills, CA; **Ian Crocker**, 8/31/82, n/a, Portland, ME, Portland, ME; **Josh Davis**, 9/1/72, San Antonio, TX, San Antonio, TX, Austin, TX; **Tom Dolan**, 9/15/75, Arlington, VA, Arlington, VA, Arlington, VA; **Nate Dusing**, 11/25/78, n/a, Villa Hills, KY, Villa Hills, KY; **Anthony Ervin**, 5/26/81, Valencia, CA, Valencia, CA, Valencia, CA; **Scott Goldblatt**, 7/12/79, Summit, NJ, Scotch Plains, NJ, Austin, TX; **Gary Hall Jr.**, 9/26/74, Cincinnati, OH, Cincinnati, OH, Phoenix, AZ; **Tommy Hannan**, 1/14/80, Baltimore, MD, Baltimore, MD, Austin, TX; **Klete Keller**, 3/21/82, Phoenix, AZ, Phoenix, AZ, Phoenix, AZ; **Lenny Krayzelburg**, 9/28/75, Odessa, Ukraine, Los Angeles, CA, Studio City, CA; **Jason Lezak**, 11/12/75, Bellflower, CA, Irvine, CA, Irvine, CA; **Tom Malchow**, 8/18/76, St Paul, MN, St Paul, MN, Ann Arbor, MI; **Ed Moses**, 6/7/80, San Bernardino, CA, Burke, VA, Burke, VA; **Aaron Peirsol**, 7/23/83, Irvine, CA, Irvine, CA, Irvine, CA; **Michael Phelps**, 06/30/85, n/a, Baltimore, MD, Baltimore, MD; **Jamie Rauch**, 8/17/79, n/a, Cincinnati, OH, Austin, TX; **Kyle Salyards**, 12/17/80, Lancaster, PA, Lancaster, PA, Lancaster, PA; **Chris Thompson**, 11/30/78, Roseburg, OR, Roseburg, OR, Roseburg, OR; **Scott Tucker**, 2/18/75, Birmingham, AL, Largo, FL, Auburn, AL; **Erik Vendt**, 1/9/81, n/a, North Easton, MA, North Easton, MA; **Neil Walker**, 6/25/76, Madison, WI, Verona, WI, Austin, TX; **Tom Wilkens**, 11/25/75, New York, NY, Middletown, NJ, Palo Alto, CA
Team Leader: Joke Marie Schubert, 7/15/52, Willemstad,

Netherlands Antilles, Surfside, CA, Surfside, CA
Asst Team Leader: Rich DeSelm, 9/28/56, Columbus, OH, Charlotte, NC, Charlotte, NC
Asst Team Leader: Susan Teeter, 6/21/59, Miami, FL, Flemington, NJ, Flemington, NJ
Women's Head Coach: Richard Quick, 1/31/43, Akron, OH, Menlo Park, CA, Menlo Park, CA
Men's Head Coach: Mark Schubert, 1/29/49, Cleveland, OH, Surfside, CA, Surfside, CA
Asst Coaches:
Jon Urbaneck, n/a, n/a, Ann Arbor, MI, n/a; **Jack Bauerle**, n/a, n/a, Athens, GA, n/a; **Ed Reese**, n/a, n/a, Austin, TX, n/a; **David Marsh**, n/a, n/a, Auburn, AL, n/a; **Dave Salo**, n/a, n/a, Lake Forest, CA, n/a; **Peter Banks**, n/a, n/a, Tampa, FL, n/a

Swimming Support Personnel:
Team Administrator: Denny Pursley, 6/19/50, Dayton, OH, Colorado Springs, CO, Colorado Springs, CO
Team Coordinator: Everett Uchiyama, 11/5/55, Pasadena, CA, Colorado Springs, CO, Colorado Springs, CO
Team Liaison: Jim Wood, 3/24/50, Jersey City, NJ, New Providence, NJ, New Providence, NJ
Race Analyst: Jonty Skinner, 2/15/54, Cape Town, South Africa, Colorado Springs, CO, Colorado Springs, CO

Synchronized Swimming
Women (9)
Name, Birth date, Birthplace, Hometown, Current Residence
Carrie Barton, 5/19/76, Dallas, TX, Irving, TX, Santa Clara, CA; **Tammy Cleland-McGregor**, 10/26/75, Sanford, FL, Orlando, FL, Oakland, CA; **Bridget Finn**, 2/2/74, Buffalo, NY, Buffalo, NY, Santa Clara, CA; **Anna Kozlova**, 12/30/72, St Petersburg, Russia, St Petersburg, Russia, Santa Clara, CA; **Kristina Lum**, 10/18/76, Santa Clara, CA, Fremont, CA, Santa Clara, CA; **Elicia Marshall**, 3/9/79, San Jose, CA, San Jose, CA, Santa Clara, CA; **Tuesday Middaugh**, 8/27/73, Riverside, CA, Riverside, CA, Santa Clara, CA; **Heather Pease-Olson**, 9/29/75, Monterey, CA, Monterey, CA, Half Moon, CA; **Kim Wurzel**, 9/18/76, San Jose, CA, Santa Clara, CA, Campbell, CA
Team Leader: Kris Olson, 8/2/48, Battle Creek, MI, Burke, VA, Burke, VA
Head Coach: Chris Carver, 2/28/42, Palo Alto, CA, Saratoga, CA, Saratoga, CA
Asst Coach: Gail Emery, 5/29/51, Oakland, CA, Lafayette, CA, Lafayette, CA

Synchronized Swimming Support Personnel:
Team Administrator: Charlotte Davis, 4/30/50, Seattle, WA, Seattle, WA, Seattle, WA
Technical Consultant: Margo Erickson, 3/23/35, Minneapolis, MN, Indianapolis, IN, Indianapolis, IN

Table Tennis
Women (4)
Name, Birth date, Birthplace, Hometown, Current Residence
Tawny Banh, 12/12/74, Bac Lieu, Vietnam, Alhambra, CA, Alhambra, CA; **Gao Jun Chang**, 1/25/69, Hebei, China, Gaithersburg, MD, Gaithersburg, MD; **Michelle Do**, 6/6/83, Sunnyvale, CA, Milpitas, CA, Milpitas, CA; **Jasna Reed**, 12/20/70, Foca, Yugoslavia, Davison, MI, Davison, MI

Men (4)
Name, Birth date, Birthplace, Hometown, Current Residence
Yinghua Cheng, 11/24/58, Sichuan, China, Germantown, MD, Germantown, MD; **Khoa Nguyen**, 10/9/66, NhaTrang, Vietnam, San Jose, CA, San Jose, CA; **Todd Sweeris**, 5/28/73, Grand Rapids, MI, Bethesda, MD, Bethesda, MD; **David Zhuang**, 9/1/63, Guondung, China, North Brunswick, NJ, North Brunswick, NJ
Team Leader: Bob Fox, 12/6/43, Minneapolis, MN, St Paul, MN, St Paul, MN
Women's Coach: Teodor Gheorghe, 6/11/52, Bucharest, Romania, Davison, MI, Davison, MI
Men's Coach: Dan Seemiller, 6/13/54, Pittsburgh, PA, New Carlisle, IN, New Carlisle, IN

Taekwondo
Women (2)
Name, Birth date, Birthplace, Hometown, Current Residence
Barbara Kunkel, 9/17/69, Tacoma, WA, Tacoma, WA, Colorado Springs, CO; **Kay Poe**, 5/15/82, Houston, TX, Houston, TX, Houston, TX

Men (2)
Name, Birth date, Birthplace, Hometown, Current Residence
Steven Lopez, 11/9/78, New York, NY, Sugarland, TX, Sugarland, TX; **Juan Moreno**, 4/1/71, Libertyville, IL, Miami, FL, Miami, FL
Team Leader: John Holloway, 11/18/50, Norfolk, VA, Washington, DC, Washington, DC
Head Coach: Young In Cheon, 11/25/54, Seoul, Korea, Diamond Bar, CA, Diamond Bar, CA
National Team Coach: Han Lee, 5/18/62, Seoul, Korea, Colorado Springs, CO, Colorado Springs, CO

Tennis
Women (4)
Lindsay Davenport, 6/8/76, Palos Verdes, CA, Palos Verdes, CA, Wesley Chapel, FL; **Monica Seles**, 12/2/73, Novi Sad, Yugoslavia, Novi Sad, Yugoslavia, Sarasota, FL; **Serena Williams**, 9/26/81, Saginaw, MI, Lynwood, CA, Palm Beach Gardens, FL; **Venus Williams**, 6/17/80, Lynwood, CA, Lynwood, CA, Palm Beach Gardens, FL

Men (6)
Michael Chang, 2/22/72, Hoboken, NJ, Hoboken, NJ, Mercer Island, WA; **Todd Martin**, 7/8/70, Hinsdale, IL, Lansing, MI, Ponte Vedra Beach, FL; **Alex O'Brien**, 3/7/70, Amarillo, TX, Amarillo, TX, Amarillo, TX; **Jared Palmer**, 7/2/71, New York, NY, New York, NY, Palo Alto, CA; **Vince Spadea**, n/a, n/a, n/a, n/a; **Jeff Tarango**, 11/20/68, Manhattan Beach, CA, Manhattan Beach, CA, Manhattan Beach, CA
Team Leader: Jackie Kuhnert, 1/25/68, Bronx, NY, Greenwich, CT, Greenwich, CT
Women's Head Coach: Billie Jean King, 11/22/43, Long Beach, CA, Chicago, IL, Chicago, IL
Men's Head Coach: Stan Smith, 12/14/46, Pasadena, CA, Hilton Head, SC, Hilton Head, SC
Women's Assistant Coach: Zina Garrison, 11/16/63, Houston, TX, Houston, TX, Houston, TX
Men's Assistant Coach: Scott McCain, n/a, n/a, n/a, n/a

Tennis Support Personnel:

Team Administrator: Jeff Ryan, 12/20/63, Red Bank, NJ, White Plains, NY, White Plains, NY

Equipment Manager: Beven Pace Livingston, 12/19/60, Lexington, KY, Lilburn, GA, Lilburn, GA

TRIATHLON

Women (3)

Name, Birth date, Birthplace, Hometown, Current Residence

Jennifer Gutierrez, 4/28/67, San Antonio, TX, San Antonio, TX, Denver, CO; **Shelia Taormina**, 3/18/69, Livonia, MI, Livonia, MI, Livonia, MI; **Joanna Zeiger**, 5/4/70, Baltimore, MD, San Diego, CA, Baltimore, MD

Men (3)

Ryan Bolton, 3/26/73, Rapid City, SD, Gillette, WY, Colorado Springs, CO; **Hunter Kemper**, 5/4/76, Charlotte, NC, Charlotte, NC, Orlando, FL; **Nick Radkewich**, 1/10/71, Royal Oak, MI, Royal Oak, MI, Colorado Springs, CO

Team Leader: Tim Yount, 9/8/64, Greeley, CO, Colorado Springs, CO, Colorado Springs, CO

Head Coach: Michelle Blessing, 10/31/63, Denver, CO, Colorado Springs, CO, Colorado Springs, CO

Triathlon Support Personnel:

Mechanic: Brian Davis, 5/13/64, n/a, Denver, CO, Denver, CO

VOLLEYBALL

BEACH

Women (4)

Name, Birth date, Birthplace, Hometown, Current Residence

Annett Davis, 9/22/73, Long Beach, CA, Long Beach, CA, Tarzana, CA; **Jennifer Johnson Jordan**, 6/8/73, Tarzana, CA, Tarzana, CA, Tarzana, CA; **Misty May**, 7/30/77, Costa Mesa, CA, Newport Beach, CA, Newport Beach, CA; **Holly McPeak**, 5/15/69, Hollywood, CA, Redondo Beach, CA, Redondo Beach, CA

Men (4)

Name, Birth date, Birthplace, Hometown, Current Residence

Dain Blanton, 11/28/71, Laguna Beach, CA, Laguna Beach, CA, Laguna Beach, CA; **Eric Fonoimoana**, 6/7/69, Torrance, CA, Hermosa Beach, CA, n/a; **Rob Heidger**, 6/3/69, Manhattan Beach, CA, Manhattan Beach, CA, Manhattan Beach, CA; **Kevin Wong**, 9/12/72, Honolulu, HI, Honolulu, HI, Playa del Rey, CA

Team Leader: John Kessel, 10/17/52, Hollywood, CA, Colorado Springs, CO, Colorado Springs, CO

Assistant Team Leader: Charles Jackson, 11/30/48, Honolulu, HI, Poway, CA, Poway, CA

Beach Volleyball Support Personnel:

Anna Biller-Collier, Gene Selznick, Dane Selznick, Greg Vernovage

INDOOR

Women (12)

Name, Birth date, Birthplace, Hometown, Current Residence

Tara Cross Battle, 9/16/68, Houston, TX, Houston, TX, n/a; **Heather Bown**, 11/29/78, n/a, Yorba Linda, CA, n/a; **Mickisha Hurley**, 3/6/75, Miami, FL, Miami, FL, n/a; **Robyn Ah Mow**, n/a, n/a, Honolulu, HI, n/a; **Sarah Noriega**, 4/24/76, n/a, Ulysses, KS, n/a; **Demetria Sance**, 8/19/77, San Antonio, TX, San Antonio, TX, n/a; **Danielle Scott**, 10/1/72, Baton Rouge, LA, Baton Rouge, LA, n/a; **Stacy Sykora**, 6/24/77, n/a, Burleson, TX, n/a; **Charlene Tagaloa**, 8/30/73, Las Vegas, NV, Las Vegas, NV, n/a; **Logan Tom**, 5/25/81, Salt Lake City, UT, Salt Lake City, UT, Palo Alto, CA; **Kerri Walsh**, n/a, n/a, Saratoga, CA, n/a; **Allison Weston**, 2/19/74, n/a, Papillion, NE, n/a

Team Leader: Robert Gambardella, 6/3/54, Staten Island, NY, Colorado Springs, CO, Colorado Springs, CO

Head Coach: Michael (Mick) Haley, 8/18/43, Angola, IN, Monument, CO, Monument, CO

Asst Coach: Jeremiah Estes, 8/24/73, Honolulu, HI, Colorado Springs, CO, Colorado Springs, CO

Asst Coach: Toshiaki Yoshida, 10/2/54, Yamagata, Japan, Colorado Springs, CO, Colorado Springs, CO

Indoor Volleyball Support Personnel:

Technical Coordinator: Monica Paul, 7/21/75, Caldwell, TX, Colorado Springs, CO, Colorado Springs, CO

Scout Coach: Jim Miret, 4/20/59, Van Nuys, CA, Denver, CO, Denver, CO

Men (12)

Name, Birth date, Birthplace, Hometown, Current Residence

Lloy Ball, 2/14/72, Fort Wayne, IN, Fort Wayne, IN, Colorado Springs, CO; **Kevin Barnett**, 5/14/74, Joliet, IL, Naperville, IL, Colorado Springs, CO; **Tom Hoff**, 6/9/73, Chicago, IL, Park Ridge, IL, Colorado Springs, CO; **John Hyden**, 10/7/72, Pensacola, FL, San Diego, CA, Colorado Springs, CO; **Mike Lambert**, 4/14/74, Honolulu, HI, Kaneohe, HI, Kaneohe, HI; **Daniel Landry**, 1/15/70, San Diego, CA, San Diego, CA, San Diego, CA; **Christian (Chip) McCaw**, 3/24/73, Chicago, IL, Tulsa, OK, Colorado Springs, CO; **Ryan Millar**, 1/22/78, San Dimas, CA, Palmdale, CA, Colorado Springs, CO; **Jeff Nygaard**, 8/3/72, Madison, WI, Madison, WI, Colorado Springs, CO; **George Roumain**, 3/28/76, Dorado, PR, Parkland, FL, Colorado Springs, CO; **Erik Sullivan**, 8/9/72, San Diego, CA, Encinitas, CA, Colorado Springs, CO; **Andy Witt**, 3/21/78, Santa Maria, CA, Santa Ynez, CA, Santa Ynez, CA

Team Leader: Jim Coleman, 10/22/31, Milwaukee, WI, Chula Vista, CA, Chula Vista, CA

Head Coach: Douglas Beal, 3/4/47, Cleveland, OH, Colorado Springs, CO, Colorado Springs, CO

Asst Coach: Marv Dunphy, 1/7/48, Santa Monica, CA, Malibu, CA, Malibu, CA

Asst Coach: Rodney Wilde, 11/4/56, Terre Haute, IN, Santee, CA, Santee, CA

Indoor Volleyball Support Personnel:

Technical Coordinator: Robert Browning, 4/19/66, Glendale, CA, Colorado Springs, CO, Colorado Springs, CO

Scout Coach: Corey Flanagan, , Denver, CO, Colorado Springs, CO

WATER POLO

Women (13)

Robin Beauregard, 2/23/79, Long Beach, CA, Huntington Beach, CA, Huntington Beach, CA; **Ellen Estes**, 10/13/78, Portland, OR, Novato, CA, Novato, CA; **Courtney Johnson**, 5/7/74, Salt Lake City, UT, Salt Lake City, UT, Salt Lake City, UT; **Ericka Lorenz**,

2000 U.S. Olympic Team Roster

2/18/81, San Diego, CA, San Diego, CA, San Diego, CA; **Heather Moody**, 8/21/73, Rexburg, ID, Green River, WY, Green River, WY; **Maureen O'Toole**, 3/24/61, Long Beach, CA, Piedmont, CA, Piedmont, CA; **Bernice Orwig**, 11/24/76, Anaheim, CA, Anaheim, CA, Anaheim, CA; **Nicolle Payne**, 7/15/76, Paramount, CA, Cerritos, CA, Cerritos, CA; **Heather Petrie**, 6/13/78, Orinda, CA, Orinda, CA, Orinda, CA; **Kathy (Gubba) Sheehy**, 4/26/70, Moraga, CA, San Diego, CA, San Diego, CA; **Coralie Simmons**, 3/1/77, Hemet, CA, Hemet, CA, Hemet, CA; **Julie Swail**, 12/27/72, Anaheim, CA, Placentia, CA, Placentia, CA; **Brenda Villa**, 4/18/80, Los Angeles, CA, Commerce, CA, Commerce, CA

Team Leader: **Michelle Pickering**, 3/28/64, Lynwood, CA, Long Beach, CA, Long Beach, CA

Head Coach: **Guy Baker**, 1/27/61, Indio, CA, Long Beach, CA, Long Beach, CA

Asst Coach: **Chris Duplanty**, 10/21/65, Palo Alto, CA, Honolulu, HI, Honolulu, HI

Asst Coach: **Ken Lindgren**, 1/19/38, Ellwood City, PA, Huntington Beach, CA, Huntington Beach, CA

Water Polo Support Personnel:

Scout Coach: **Rachael Scott**, n/a, n/a, n/a, n/a

Men (13)

Gavin Arroyo, 5/10/72, Orange, CA, Orange, CA, Orange, CA; **Tony Azevedo**, 11/21/81, Rio de Janeiro, Brazil, Long Beach, CA, Long Beach, CA; **Ryan Bailey**, 8/28/75, Long Beach, CA, Long Beach, CA, Long Beach, CA; **Dan Hackett**, 9/11/70, Syracuse, NY, Irvine, CA, Irvine, CA; **Chris Humbert**, 12/27/69, Modesto, CA, Lodi, CA, Lodi, CA; **Sean Kern**, 7/11/78, n/a, Honolulu, HI, n/a; **Kyle Kopp**, 11/10/66, San Bernardino, CA, San Bernardino, CA, San Bernardino, CA; **Craig (Chi) Kredell**, 2/16/71, Long Beach, CA, Seal Beach, CA, Seal Beach, CA; **Robert Lynn**, 2/7/67, Long Beach, CA, Long Beach, CA, Long Beach, CA; **Sean Nolan**, 7/18/72, Palo Alto, CA, Palo Alto, CA, Palo Alto, CA; **Chris Oeding**, 9/11/70, Santa Ana, CA, Newport Beach, CA, Newport Beach, CA; **Brad Schumacher**, 3/6/74, Bowie, MD, Bowie, MD, Bowie, MD; **Wolf Wigo**, 3/6/74, Abington, PA, New York, NY, New York, NY

Team Leader: **Barbara Kalbus**, 9/3/31, Superior, WI, Newport Beach, CA, Newport Beach, CA

Head Coach: **John Vargus**, 6/17/61, Fullerton, CA, Newport Beach, CA, Newport Beach, CA

Asst Coach: **Monte Nitzkowski**, 9/7/29, Pasadena, CA, Huntington Beach, CA, Huntington Beach, CA

Asst Coach: **John Tanner**, 7/13/60, Stanford, CA, Stockton, CA, Stockton, CA

Water Polo Support Personnel:

Scout Coach: **Bill Barnett**, 8/31/42, Los Angeles, CA, Laguna Beach, CA, Laguna Beach, CA

WEIGHTLIFTING

Women (4)

Robin Goad, 1/17/70, Newnan, GA, Newnan, GA, Newnan, GA; **Cheryl Haworth**, 4/19/83, Savannah, GA, Savannah, GA, Savannah, GA; **Cara Heads-Lane**, 10/7/77, Costa Mesa, CA, Costa Mesa, CA, Savannah, GA; **Tara Nott**, 5/10/72, n/a, Stilwell, KS, Colorado Springs, CO

Men (2)

Oscar Chaplin III, 2/22/80, Savannah, GA, Savannah, GA,

Savannah, GA; **Shane Hamman**, 6/20/72, Oklahoma City, OK, Mustang, OK, Colorado Springs, CO

Team Leader: **Roger Sadecki**, 12/5/42, Minneapolis, MN, Roseville, MN, Roseville, MN

Men's Coach: **Dragomir Cioroslan**, 5/15/59, Cluj, Romania, Colorado Springs, CO, Colorado Springs, CO

Women's Coach: **Michael Cohen**, 1/28/58, Savannah, GA, Savannah, GA, Savannah, GA

WRESTLING

FREESTYLE (8)

Name, Birth date, Birthplace, Hometown, Current Residence

Terry Brands, 4/9/68, Omaha, NE, Sheldon, IA, Lincoln, NE; **Charles Burton**, 10/9/73, Ontario, OR, Meridian, ID, Bloomington, IN; **Melvin Douglas**, 8/21/63, Topeka, KS, Topeka, KS, Mesa, AZ; **Samuel Henson**, 1/1/71, St Charles, MO, St Louis, MO, Norman, OK; **Cary Kolat**, 5/19/73, Rice's Landing, PA, Rice's Landing, PA, Morgantown, WV; **Kerry McCoy**, 8/2/74, Riverhead, NY, Middle Island, NY, State College, PA; **Lincoln McIlravy**, 7/17/74, Philip, SD, Rapid City, SD,, Iowa City, IA; **Brandon Slay**, 10/14/75, Amarillo, TX, Amarillo, TX, Colorado Springs, CO

Team Leader: **Scott Beck**, 5/19/58, Illinois, Boulder, CO, Boulder, CO

National Team Coach: **Bruce Burnett**, 9/15/49, Modesto, CA, Bakersfield, CA, Colorado Springs, CO

Freestyle Support Personnel:

Co-Coach: **Dan Gable**, 10/25/48, Waterloo, IA,, Iowa City, IA,, Iowa City, IA

Co-Coach: **John Smith**, 9/8/65, Oklahoma City, OK, Del City, OK, Stillwater, OK

Co-Coach: **Greg Strobel**, 8/17/52, Terry, MT, Scappoose, OR, Bethlehem, PA

GRECO-ROMAN (8)

Name, Birth date, Birthplace, Hometown, Current Residence

Kevin Bracken, 10/29/71, Chicago, IL, Chicago, IL, Colorado Springs, CO; **Quincey Clark**, 6/5/72, Norman, OK, San Diego, CA, New Brighton, MN; **Rulon Gardner**, 8/16/71, Afton, WY, Afton, WY, Colorado Springs, CO; **James (Jim) Gruenwald**, 6/9/70, Milwaukee, WI, Milwaukee, WI, Colorado Springs, CO; **Garrett Lowney**, 10/3/79, Appleton, WI, Appleton, WI, Minneapolis, MN; **Steven Mays**, 6/17/66, Kalamazoo, MI, Kalamazoo, MI, Pensacola, FL; **Matt Lindland**, 5/17/70, Oregon City, OR, Gladstone, OR, Lincoln, NE; **Heath Sims**, 10/14/71, Orange, CA, Irvine, CA, Huntington Beach, CA

Team Leader: **Tom Press**, 1/21/56, Fargo, ND, Minnetonka, MN, Minnetonka, MN

Head Coach: **Dan Chandler**, 11/29/51, Minneapolis, MN, Minneapolis, MN, Minneapolis, MN

Greco-Roman Support Personnel:

National Team Coach: **Steve Fraser**, 3/23/58, Detroit, MI, Colorado Springs, CO, Colorado Springs, CO

Assistant Coach: **Rob Hermann**, 1/15/57, Chicago, IL, Pensacola, FL, Pensacola, FL

Assistant Coach: **Jay Antonelli**, , Quantico, VA, Quantico, VA

Total Number of US Athletes - 602

2000 U.S. Olympic Team

Teresa M. Costello   Janet Dykman   Nancy E. Myrick   Denise Parker   Karen Scavotto

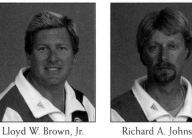     

Lloyd W. Brown, Jr.   Richard A. Johnson   Rodney White   Victor S. Wunderle   Athletics   Amy Acuff

Erin Aldrich   Andrea Anderson   Mikele Barber   Kim Batten   Kelly Blair-LaBounty   Lynda Blutreich

  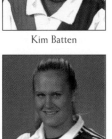  

Tonja Buford-Bailey   Dawn Burrell   Sheila Burrell   Emily Carlsten   Yueling Chen   Christine Clark

Hazel Clark   Joetta Clark-Diggs   Latasha Colander-Richardson   Michelle Collins   Jesseca Cross   Karol Damon

Stacy Dragila   Deena Drossin   Elva Dryer   Dawn Dumble   Dawn Ellerbe   Suzy Favor Hamilton

Sandy Fowler   Chryste Gaines   Nicole Gamble   Sandra Glover   Judy Harrison   Monique Henderson

2000 U.S. Olympic Team

 Monique Hennagan

 Libbie Hickman

 Shakedia Jones

 Kristin Kuehl

 Anne Marie Lauck

 Debbi Lawrence

 Jearl Miles-Clark

 Melissa Morrison

 Melissa Mueller

 DeDee Nathan

 Amy Palmer

 Nanceen Perry

 Suzy Powell

 Connie Price-Smith

 Mamie Rallins

 Jennifer Rhines

 Passion Richardson

 Michelle Rohl

 Amy Rudolph

 Marla Runyan

 Rita Somerlot

 Seilala Sua

 Kellie Suttle

 LaVerne Sweat

 Teri Tunks

 Shana Williams

 Abdi Abdirahmen

 Charles Austin

 Andy Bloom

 Dick Booth

 Kenneth Brokenburr

 John Capel

 James Carter

 LaMark Carter

 John Chaplin

 Curt Clausen

 Mike Conley

 Tony Cosey

 Mark J. Crear

 Mark Croghan

 Alan Culpepper

 Walter Davis

2000 U.S. Olympic Team

Lance Deal

Rodney P. Dehaven

Pascal Dobert

Jon Drummond

Philip Dunn

Kenny W. Evans

Mark Everett

Dixon Farmer

John Godina

Adam Goucher

Maurice Greene

Breaux Greer

Ernie Gregoire

Alvin Harrison

Calvin Harrison

Chad Harting

Brad Hauser

Floyd Heard

Keith Henschen

Andrew Hermann

Ja'Warren Hooker

Robert P. Howard

Chris Huffins

Nick Hysong

Kip Javrin

Gabe Jennings

Allen Johnson

Curtis Johnson

Lawrence Johnson

Michael Johnson

Rob Johnson

Meb Keflezghi

Rich Kenah

Nathan Leeper

Melvin Lister

Danny McCray

Kevin McMahon

Coby Miller

Tim Montgomery

John Moon

Adam Nelson

Fred Newhouse

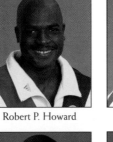

259

2000 U.S. Olympic Team

Tom Pappas

Andrew Pettigrew

Dwight Phillips

Jason Pyrah

Jerry Quiller

Nick Rogers

Tim Seaman

Adam Setliff

L. Jay Silvester

Michael Stember

Savante Stringfellow

Angelo Taylor

Eric Thomas

Bubba Thornton

Terrence Trammell

Anthony Washington

Bryan Woodward

Bernard Williams

Jerome Young

BADMINTON

Kevin Han

Stephen Kearney

Ardy Wiranata

BASEBALL

Brent Abernathy

Kurt Ainsworth

Pat Borders

Dick Cooke

Travis Dawkins

Adam Everett

Chris George

Shane Hearns

Marcus Jensen

Mike Kinkade

Rick Krivda

Tom Lasorda

Doug Mienkiewicz

Mike Neill

Jon Rauch

Phil Regan

Eddie Rodriquez

Anthony Sanders

2000 U.S. Olympic Team

Bobby Seay

Paul Seiler

Ben Sheets

Reggie Smith

Ray Tanner

Brad Wilkerson

Todd Williams

Ernie Young

Tim Young

BASKETBALL

Carol L. Callan

Teresa Edwards

Nell A. Fortner

Peggie Gillom

Yolanda E. Griffith

Chamique Holdsclaw

Ruthie Bolton-Holifield

Lisa Leslie

Nikki K. McCray

Delisha Milton

Katherine M. Smith

Dawn M. Staley

Sheryl D. Swoopes

Natalie Williams

Kara E. Wolters

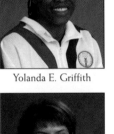
Shareef Abdur-Rahim

Ray Allen

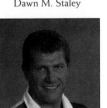
Geno Auriemma

Vincent L. Baker

Larry Brown

Vincent L. Carter

Kevin Garnett

Tim Hardaway

Allan Houston

Lloyd E. Keady

Jason F. Kidd

Antonio McDyess

Alonzo Mourning

Gary D. Payton

Tubby Smith

Steven D. Smith

Rudolph Tomjanovich

261

2000 U.S. Olympic Team

James Tooley

BOXING

Isreal Acosta

Olanda Anderson

Michael Bennett

Calvin Brock

Dante Craig

David Jackson

Ricardo Juarez

Jeffrey Lacy

Candelario Lopez

Tom Mustin

Jose Navarro

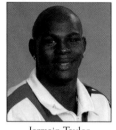

Jermain Taylor

Gary Toney

Brian Viloria

Clarence Vinson

Ricardo Williams

CANOE/ KAYAK

Rebecca Bennett-Giddens

Katheryn Colin

Jennifer Hearn

Tamara Jenkins

Philippe Boccara

Bob Campbell

Jerzy Dziadkowiec

Eric Giddens

Lecky Haller

David Hearn

Stein Jorgensen

Mike Lewis

Jordan Malloch

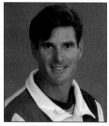

Cliff Meidl

John Mooney

Peter Newton

Angel Perez

Silvan Poberaj

Scott Shipley

Rafel Smolen

Matt Taylor

Howard Turner

2OOO U.S. OLYMPIC TEAM

CYCLING

 Alison Dunlap

 Nicole Freedman

 Mari Holden

 Karen Kurreck

 Tanya Lindenmuth

Ruth Matthes

 Erin Mirabella

 Henny Topp

 Ann Trombley

Christine Witty

Christian Arrue

John Bairos

Derek Bouchard-Hall

Travis Brown

 Jame Carney

 Jonas Carney

Desmond Dickie

 Mariano Fredrick

Stephane Girard

 Craig Griffin

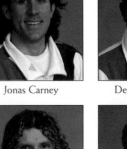 Erin Hartwell

 David Juarez

 Jiri Mainus

 Thomas Mulkey

 Martin Nothstein

 Sean Petty

 DIVING

 Michelle Davidson

 Jennifer Keim

 Sara Reiling

 Laura Wilkinson

 Randolph Ableman

 Kenneth Armstrong

 Van Austin

 Troy Dumias

 Jeffrey Huber

 Patrick Jeffrey

 John Lerew

 Timothy O'Brien

 David Pichler

 Mark Ruiz

2000 U.S. Olympic Team

Mathew Scoggin

EQUESTRIAN

Julie Black

Susan Blinks

Nina Fout

Nona Garson

Margie Goldstein-Engle

Lauren Hough

Sara Ike

Laura Kraut

Karen O'Conner

Maureen Pethick

Jessica Ransehausen

Christine Traurig

Linden Wiesman

Robert Costello

Frank Chapot

Robert Dover

David O'Conner

Mark Phillips

Guenter Seidel

Jim Wolf

FENCING

Ann Marsh

Carla Mae Richards

Arlene Stevens

Felicia Zimmerman

Iris Zimmerman

Clifford Bayer

Tamir Bloom

Carl Borack

Robert Largman

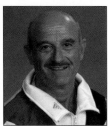
Anthony Leach

Yeftin Litvan

Keeth Smart

Akhnaten Spencer-El

GYMNASTICS

Amy Chow

Jamie Dantzcher

Dominique Dawes

Kelli Hill

Kathy Kelley

2000 U.S. Olympic Team

Kristin Maloney

Elise Ray

Tasha Shcwikert

Mary Tracy

Ron Galimore

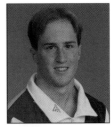

Morgan Hamm

Paul Hamm

Bela Karolyi

Peter Kormann

Stephen McCain

John Roethlisberger

Stephen Rybacki

Yoichi Tomita

Sean Townsend

Barry Weiner

Blaine Wilson

JUDO

Sandra Bacher

Lauren Meece

Coleen Rosensteel

Celita Schutz

Ellen Wilson

Hillary Wolf

Martin Boonzaayer

Steve Cohen

James Colgan

Evelio Garcia

Brandon Greczkowski

Ato Hand

Edward Liddie

Jason Morris

Lou Moyerman

Brian Olson

Alexander Ottiano

James Pedro

MODERN
PENTATHLON

Shane Brashar

Emily de Riel

Mary Larsen

Jim Gregory

Vakh Igorashvili

Velizar Iliev

2000 U.S. Olympic Team

Janusz Peciak   Chad Senior   Viktor Svatenko

ROWING

Christine Collins   Ruth Davidon

Jennifer Dore-Terhaar   Torrey Folk   Amy Fuller   Sarah Garner   Hilary Gehman   Sarah Jones

Laurel Korholz   Karen Kraft   Katie Maloney   Amy Martin   Betsy McCagg   Linda Miller

Lianne Nelson   Missy Ryan   Kelley Salchow   Rajanya Shah   Carol Skricki   Monica Tranel-Michini

   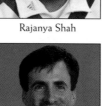  

Christian Ahrens   Thomas Auth   Sebastian Bea   Willie Black   Peter Cipollone   Porter Collins

Michael Ferry   Conal Groom   Michael Hall   Bob Kaehler   Jeffrey Klepacki   James Koven

  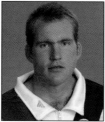  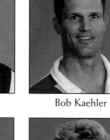  

Ian McGowan   Garret Miller   Wolfgang Moser   Eric Mueller   Ted Murphy   Henry Nuzum

2000 U.S. Olympic Team

 Nicholas Peterson

 Gregory Ruckman

 Marcus Schnieder

 David Simon

 Don Smith

 Mark Sniderman

 Steve Tucker

 Bryan Volpenhein

 Tom Welsh

 Jake Wetzel

 Michael Wherley

SAILING

 Lanee Butler

 Courtenay Becker-Dey

 Sarah Glaser

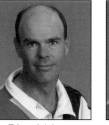 Edward Adams

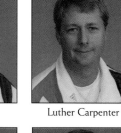 Gary Bodie

 Luther Carpenter

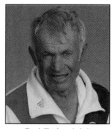 Carl Eichenlalub

 Paul Foerster

 Jay Glaser

 Hal Haenel

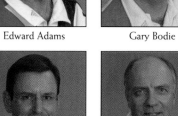 Jonathon Harley

 Craig Healy

 Pierre Jeangirard

 Hartwell Jordan

 Magnus Liljedahl

 John Lovell

 Jefferey Madrigali

 Charles McKee

 Robert Merrik

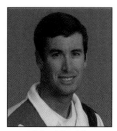 John Myrdal

 Charles Ogletree

 Mark Reynolds

 Russell Silvestri

 Skip White

 James Worthington

SHOOTING

 Janine Bowman

 Christina Cassidy

 Jayme Dickman

 Jean Foster

267

2000 U.S. Olympic Team

Margot Jonker

Jennifer McFalls

Stacy Nuveman

Leah O'Brien-Amico

Dot Richardson

Michele Smith

Shirley Topley

Michelle Venturella

Christa Williams

Ralph Raymond

Ralph Weekly

SWIMMING

Amanda J. Adkins

Samantha Arsenault

Amanda Beard

Barbara J. Bedford

Lindsay Benko

Brooke Bennett

Kim Black

Madeleine Crippen

Misty D. Hyman

Kristina A. Kowal

Diana M. Munz

Rada E. Owen

Erin Phenix

Megan M. Quann

Gabrielle E. Rose

Kaitlin S. Sandeno

Joke M. Schubert

Courtney A. Shealy

Staciana Stitts

Julia G. Stowers

Ashley T. Tappin

Susan S. Teeter

Cristina Teuscher

Jenny B. Thompson

Dara G. Torres

Amy D. Van Dyken

Peter Banks

John Baurle

Pat Calhoun

Chad Carvin

2000 U.S. Olympic Team

Ian L. Crocker

Josh C. Davis

Richard L. Deselm

Tom F. Dolan

Nate J. Dusing

Anthony L. Ervin

Scott D. Goldblatt

Gary Hall, Jr.

Tommy Hannan

Klete D. Keller

Lenny Krayzelburg

Jason E. Lezak

Tom A. Malchow

David Marsh

Ed Moses

Aaron W. Peirsol

Michael Phelps

Richard W. Quick

Jamie R. Rauch

Ed C. Reese

David C. Salo

Mark K. Salyards

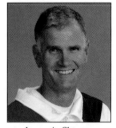
Mark E. Schubert

Jonty A. Skinner

Christopher L. Thompson

Scott E. Tucker

Everett K. Uchiyama

Jon C. Urbanchek

Erik K. Vendt

Neil S. Walker

Tom P. Wilkens

James Woods

Synchronized Swimming

Carrie Barton

Christine Carver

Tammy Cleland-McGregor

Gail Emery

Bridget Finn

Anna Kozlova

Kristina Lum

Elicia Marshall

Tuesday Middaugh

2000 U.S. Olympic Team

Kristine Olson

Heather Pease-Olson

Kimberly Wurzel

TABLE TENNIS

Tawny A. Banh

Gao Jun Chang

Michelle Do

Jasna Reed

Yinghua Cheng

Bob Fox

Teodor Gheorghe

Khoa Nguyen

Daniel Seemiller

Todd Sweeris

David Zhuang

TAEKWONDO

Barbara Kunkel

Kay Poe

Young Cheon

John Holloway

Han Lee

Steven Lopez

Juan Moreno

TENNIS

Lindsay Davenport

Billie Jean King

Jacqueline Kuhnert

Monica Seles

Serena Williams

Venus Williams

Michael Chang

Todd Martin

Alex O'Brien

Jared Palmer

Stan Smith

Vince Spadea

Jeff Tarango

TRIATHLON

Michelle Blessing

Jennifer Gutierrez

Sheila Taormina

Joanna Zeiger

2000 U.S. Olympic Team

Ryan Bolton

Brian Davis

Hunter Kemper

Nick Radkewich

Tim Yount

Robyn Ah Mow

Heather Bown

Anna Collier

Tara Cross-Battle

Annett Davis

Mickisha Hurley

Jennifer Johnson-Jordan

Misty May

Holly McPeak

Sarah Noriega

Demetria Sance

Danielle Scott

Stacy Sykora

Charlene Tagaloa

Logan Tom

Kerri Walsh

Allison Weston

Kevin Barnett

Douglas Beal

Dain Blanton

James Coleman

Robert Gambardella

Marvin Dunphy

Jeremiah Estes

Eric Fonoimoana

Michael Haley

Robert Heidger

Tom Hoff

John Hyden

Charlie Jackson

John Kessel

Michael Lambert

Daniel Landry

Christian McCaw

Ryan Millar

Jeff Nygaard

273

2000 U.S. Olympic Team

George Roumain

Dane Selznick

Eugene Selznick

Erik Sullivan

Gregory Vernovage

Rodney Wilde

Andy Witt

Kevin Wong

Toshiaki Yoshoda

WATER POLO

Robin Beauregard

Ellen Estes

Courtney Johnson

Barbara Kalbus

Erika Lorenz

Heather Moody

Maureen O'Toole

Bernice Orwig

Nicolle Payne

Heather Petri

Michelle Pickering

Rachel Scott

Katherine Sheehy

Coralie Simmons

Julie Swail

Brenda Villa

Gavin Arroyo

Anthony Azevedo

Ryan Bailey

Guy Baker

Christopher Duplanty

Daniel Hackett

Chris Humbert

Sean Kern

Kyle Kopp

Chi Kredell

Kenneth Lindgren

Robert Lynn

Monte Nitzkowski

Sean Nolan

Chris Oeding

Bradley Schumacher

2000 U.S. Olympic Team

John Tanner

John Vargas

Wolfgang Wigo

WEIGHTLIFTING

Robin Goad

Cheryl Haworth

Cara Heads-Lane

Tara Nott

Oscar Chaplin III

Dragomir Cioroslan

Michael Cohen

Shane Hamman

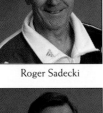
Roger Sadecki

WRESTLING

Jay Antonelli

Scott Beck

Kevin Bracken

Terry Brands

Bruce Burnett

Charles Burton

Daniel Chandler

Quincey Clark

Melvin Douglas

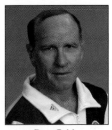
Dan Gable

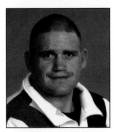
Rulon Gardner

James Gruenwald

Samuel Henson

Cary Kolat

Matt Lindland

Garrett Lowney

Steven Mays

Kerry McCoy

Lincoln McIlravy

Heath Sims

Brandon Slay

John Smith

Gregory Strobel

The following athletes participated in the 2000 Olympic Games
as part of Team USA but were unavailable for photograph:
Archery: Victor S. Wunderle; *Athletics*: Sharon Couch, Shayne Culpepper, Gail Devers, Torri Edwards,
Marion Jones, Brian Lewis, Tim Montgomery; *Badminton*: John Cotton; *Baseball*: Sean Burroughs, Roy Oswalt; *Cycling*: Lance Armstrong,
Dylan Casey, Antonio Cruz, Tyler Hamilton, George Hincapie, Fred Rodriguez, Christian Vande Velde; *Gymnastics*: Jennifer Parilla;
Judo: Amy Tong; *Rowing*: Paul Teti; *Sailing*: Jennifer Isler, Michael Gebhard, Jonathan McKee; *Volleyball*: Lloy Ball.

Athlete head shots courtesy of Long Photography, Inc., Los Angeles, CA.

USA OLYMPIC DELEGATION MEDIA SERVICES STAFF

Left-to-right (front row): Craig Miller, Tommy Sheppard, Susan Polakoff-Shaw, Brian Eaton, Seth Pederson, Nick Inzerello, Bill Kellick, Tori Svenningson, Gavin Markovitz, Randy Walker, Rich Wanninger, Irv Moss, Bob Condron, B.J. Hoeptner, Linda Luchetti, Bill Hancock. (top row) Shilpa Bakre, Cecil Blieker, Brett Johnson, Matt Farrell, Mary Wagner, Caroline Williams, Gary Abbott, Eric Velazquez, Lisa Fish, Jill Geer, Gail Dent, Christie Hyde, Jeff Howard, Melissa Minker, Dave Fannuchi, Mike Wilson.

USA OLYMPIC DELEGATION MEDICAL STAFF

Left-to-right (front row): Margaret Hunt, ATC, Dave Walden, MD, Gwyneth Short, ATC, Joe "Rigo" Carbajal, ATC, Socrates Cara, ATC, Chrissy Price, ATC, Patricia Ponce, ATC, Michael Braid, ATC, Brock Schnebel, MD; (middle row) Katherine Taylor, ATC, Angela Wheeler, MD, Michael Wilkinson, ATC, Thomas Abdenour, ATC, Vincent Comiskey, ATC, John Behrens, ATC, Brent Rich, MD, Karen Griffen, ATC, Renee Lehman, ATC, Debra Runkle, ATC, Paul Stricker, MD, Michael Burns, MD, Edward Ryan, ATC; (back row) David Weinstein, MD, Timothy Hosea, MD, Mark Adams, MD, James Robinson, MD, James Miller, ATC,Emery Hill, ATC, David Kuhn, ATC, Martin Anderegg, ATC, Debra Belcher, ATC, Andy Klein, DC, Scott Farnsworth, ATC, Scott Sunderland, ATC.

USA OLYMPIC DELEGATION HEADQUARTERS STAFF

Left-to-right (front row): Greg Harney, Faith Triggs, Tina Mendleta, Frank Aires, John Bourbonals, Joe Walton, Virginia Witte, Becky Autry, Dottie Saling, Simon Mosley, Jason Largey, David Coffey, Josh Bailey, Roger Kerr. (top row) Larry Buendorf, Kathy Menck, Chris Vadala, Chuck Patti, Ron Karolick, Carol Williams, Keith Ferguson, Diana Sherman, Kim Bartkowski, Stephanie Barr, Jason Mattas, Mark Druelinger, Mark Mager.

PACHYDERM PRESS STAFF

Left-to-right: Kim Koenemann, Associate Editor; Brad Sinclair, Operations Manager; Doug Looney, Writer; Wallace Sears, Editor/Publisher; Fran Henderson, Coordinator.

AMERICA DOESN'T SEND ITS ATHLETES TO THE OLYMPIC GAMES. . . .

AMERICANS DO.